So, What's Your Play?

HOW BILLIE JEAN, BOBBY, AND BLINDNESS BEGAT TOLERANCE

Richard J. Muscio

So, What's Your Play?
How Billie Jean, Bobby, and Blindness Begat Tolerance

Copyright © 2013 by Richard J. Muscio

Sherpa Press
1621 Central Avenue
Cheyenne, WY 82001

Sherpa Press books may be purchased for educational, business, or sales promotional use. For information, please write:
Special Markets
Sherpa Press
1621 Central Avenue
Cheyenne, WY 82001

First Edition

Library of Congress Cataloging-in-Publication Data

ISBN: 978-1-939078-17-9

eISBN: 978-1939078-00-1

Contents

Foreword

Rarely have words jumped off a page and impacted me the way this book has.

Told from an insider's point of view, this simple and easy-to-read narrative takes you along a voyeuristic journey of how a young man's life was challenged and inspired by the legendary Bobby Riggs.

Going beyond the surface of controversy, this book takes a deep dive into the lessons learned and wisdoms gained from the year that changed the world.

Not only is Richard a gifted storyteller, he is a historian of sorts.

Being an avid tennis enthusiast, his behind-the-scenes encounters will take you along the roller-coaster ride known as the Battle of the Sexes, and will surely ignite a memory or two as you flip through these historic pages.

Read for yourself, your friends, and those you love most–
I recommend it highly!

Greg S. Reid, best-selling author of *Three Feet From Gold,*
Napoleon Hill's Road to Riches, and *Think and Grow Rich:*
Stickability.

Acknowledgements

This is, after all, a book about collaboration, and without collaboration, this project would still be but an idea in my over-crowded brain.

A huge thank you goes to my seventeen-year-old daughter Demi, a high school senior who read and made suggestions on countless editions of this book, all the while managing to get straight A's during her junior year. Of course the same goes to the rest of my family, Mia, Evan and Mari, but in their case, for putting up with me and with all of the changes brought on by my tackling this project. And lest I not forget, a huge thank you goes to my mother Dolores, because after all, she finished Bobby Riggs' final scrapbook for me.

I also thank Lorne Kuhle, proprietor of the Bobby Riggs Tennis Club and the Bobby Riggs Tennis Museum Foundation, for carrying on Bobby's legacy, and for doing such a wonderful job of maintaining my handiwork.

Of course, there would have been no book at all without my great publisher Allyn Reid at Sherpa Press. Also, I wish to express my gratitude to her team, including Greg Reid,

Patti McKenna, and Bill Crawford, especially for putting up with my constant artistic demands.

Ditto for my radio show producer Joe Vecchio and our www.iymoney.com website superstar Courtney Lawver.

Most of all, I express my deepest gratitude to the wonderful Board of the Move Your Feet Before You Eat Foundation: Kathy Kinane, Gary Nessim, David Cain, Ruben Sandoval, Gerry Martin, Roger Martin, and our newest member Dr. Merrily Poth, and as well as to our hundreds of volunteers. When you combine physical activity and healthy eating with a spirit of collaboration and community involvement, well, I can only say you all have made a huge difference in our community by making it a healthier and more tolerant place.

Introduction

Today

I am writing this during the first week of Wimbledon in June 2013, and the tennis news from London arrives non-stop. Rafael Nadal loses in the first round, next defending champion Roger Federer is upset in the second round. Slippery courts are causing players to fall and sustain injuries. Victoria Azarenka slips and injures herself in her first-round win, then had to default. Maria Sharapova falls three times, contributing to her second-round ouster.

I also read, when not distracted from my professional work by tennis news, how during this same week the Supreme Court struck down significant pieces of the Defense of Marriage Act (DOMA), and sided with same-sex marriage survivor Edith Windsor on her estate tax equality matter. The Supreme Court's decisions mean that same-sex, legally married (under state law) couples can now file joint income tax returns, benefit from the Estate Tax Unlimited Marital Deduction, and receive Social Security survivor benefits… just like the rest of married American citizens.

However, the article that attracts my attention the most is about an exchange between two tennis players, one female and one male. Women's number one- ranked Serena Williams and men's number two- ranked Andy Murray, the British tennis hero, agree that a Serena versus Andy match would be entertaining for tennis fans to witness. Both players also acknowledge how lopsided the final result would be, unless Serena was granted some sort of rules advantage, like being able to hit into the doubles alleys, or allowing Andy only one serve. Yes, they agree, this would be fun and entertaining for everyone involved, and there would be no pressure involved, because the match's outcome wouldn't even matter.

"This has been done before," I remark to myself. I know Serena knows this, because of her friendship with Billie Jean King. I wonder if Andy Murray knows anything about this part of tennis history.

Indeed, 40 years ago, this man versus woman tennis drama was played in front of the entire world, twice actually, but back in 1973 it wasn't done for fun or entertainment. No, 40 years ago, the two matches were much more serious than what Serena and Andy propose. In fact, both matches were much more serious than tennis matches are supposed to be… because of what those earlier participants were trying to prove.

And unlike today's tennis and Supreme Court news, which I access with a touch of my finger, the news in 1973 travelled much more slowly, and existed primarily in paper form. In fact, the news back then existed in so much paper that it consumed the first two years of my high school life, and literally buried me with its considerable weight.

I conclude that the Supreme Court's DOMA news and what happened 40 years ago in the tennis world are essentially the same story, about how every person on this planet is entitled to the same thing: the opportunity to be whoever they really are. Read on, and you will understand why.

Chapter 1

"Okay Kid, Double or Nothing. So, What's Your Play?"

When I walked into his hotel room at the La Jolla Beach and Tennis Club almost forty years ago, Bobby Riggs was in the midst of a fierce poker game with fellow tennis greats Lew Hoad and the two Panchos—Segura and Gonzalez. Barely acknowledging my presence, Bobby glanced at me and said, "Just a minute, kid, let us finish our game." Bobby, then fifty-five years old, always called me "kid," which could have been how he referred to anyone my age. And, when I was in his company, I was invariably the youngest person in the room.

I obliged and waited patiently for the three men to finish their game. I was a fifteen-year-old high school sophomore at the time, and I had been hired by Bobby to create a set of scrapbooks. It hadn't been a small job. I spent almost 1,000 hours going through thousands of newspapers, magazines and tennis programs, reviewing, cutting and pasting articles about Bobby Riggs. The completed product was made up of 2,500 pages in eleven oversized, glossy, covered scrapbooks. After almost one year of work, I was done, and I wanted to collect the $500 balance Bobby owed me.

The game finally ended, and Pancho Gonzalez scooped the money off the table and put it in his pocket. Bobby rose from his chair and shook my hand. Nodding to the scrapbooks, he asked me to put them on the bed, but he didn't offer to pay me.

The poker game was over, but the betting apparently wasn't. Bobby smiled and made me a proposition. "Okay, kid," he said, "double or nothing. So, what's your play?"

—ᴍ—

This is the story of how a fourteen- and then fifteen-year-old boy learned how to play the game of life by putting together the scrapbooks of Bobby Riggs. Of all the lessons I learned from Bobby—tennis Hall-of-Famer, notorious gambler and hustler, self-indulgent egomaniac and self-proclaimed "king of male chauvinist pigs" during the women's liberation movement—one lesson stands out as the most important, and the most ironic: Bobby Riggs served as a catalyst for reducing intolerance. Putting together his scrapbooks taught me that the main challenge facing all of us, and our country, is that of building tolerant communities.

Although I could not know all of that at such a young age back in 1973, working on Bobby's scrapbooks also taught me the importance of taking action, collaborating and leaving a legacy. In this book, I will show you how my task taught me those skills, how these skills have affected my life and how you can use them to transform your own community.

Without question, I have benefited from everything I learned while creating Bobby's scrapbooks. I went on to build a successful career as a certified public accountant and am blessed with a wonderful wife and family. I took up tennis in 1980 and enjoyed athletic success, before blindness opened my eyes and my soul to the world around me. In 2004, I reinvented myself as a long-distance endurance runner, and then co-founder of the Move Your Feet Before You Eat Foundation.

I doubt I would have been able to achieve all that I currently have without the experience of working on those scrapbooks. That task allowed me to look deeply into the character and motivation of one of the most impressive athletes of the twentieth century. I didn't know Bobby just like a fan knows a celebrity. I knew him from thousands of articles, hundreds of interviews and hours of film. I watched his matches in detail. I processed this information with a single-minded, obsessive focus. While other kids collected baseball cards (well, I did that, too) or learned about dinosaurs (this was before the age of video games and cable TV), I had the unique, invaluable opportunity to learn about a man and a legend. It was more than a lesson in history; it was a lesson in life.

Okay, but how will the experiences of a teenage boy relate to you? First, you will learn that history is not always what it seems. The Bobby Riggs portrayed in the press is not the real Bobby Riggs, or, at least, not entirely. But, I am not interested in rewriting his story. Writers have devoted hundreds of thousands of words to telling it, in such books as *The Last Sure Thing* by Tom LeCompte, *A Necessary Spectacle* by Selena Roberts, and *Pressure Is a Privilege* by Billie Jean King. Bobby himself added his own perspective in his autobiographies, *Tennis Is My Racket* and *Court Hustler*. What I will do is cut through the fog that surrounds Bobby's story, dispel the myths and illuminate the many reasons he was truly a great man who made truly great contributions to American culture. What drove him to become a champion? What was the real story behind his challenge to Billie Jean King? What was the greatest match of his career? (The answer to this last question is a match you've probably never heard of.) As you read my story, you will learn the answers to these questions and get a completely new perspective on the life of Bobby Riggs, from the naïvely insightful perspective of fourteen-year-old boy.

When I finished the scrapbooks and delivered them to Bobby's hotel room, I had no way of knowing that my job wasn't done. The events of 1973, in the world and in tennis, would ultimately have a profound impact on my life, and, more than thirty years later, I would again be called into action—this time not to preserve the professional accomplishments of someone's life, but instead to change the lives of many.

Since 2006, I have dedicated my life to building a charitable foundation that promotes physical fitness, healthy eating and community collaboration and volunteerism. The Move Your Feet Before You Eat Foundation hosts the Oceanside Turkey Trot every Thanksgiving morning. This event features a five-mile run, a 5K run and a series of kids' one-milers and quarter-milers. This past Thanksgiving, in our seventh annual event—well, I'll put it this way: If you think you had a lot of people over for Thanksgiving, I probably have you beat. We hosted more than 9,000 runners and 14,000 people at our finish-line expo, and we assisted in the raising of more than $100,000 for charities in our community.

I was the man for the job, they said, because nearly four decades earlier, I had been Bobby Riggs' scrapbook maker.

Chapter 2

The Great Match That Wasn't

It was a typical day a few weeks before Easter of 1973 when the call came. My mother answered with her usual "Hello?" but her tone quickly turned familiar. She chatted for a few minutes with the caller, then summoned me and handed me the phone.

"Dick!" One word and I already knew who was on the line. Uncle John. The booming voice was a dead giveaway. "I've got a problem that you've got to help me with."

I was confused and a little bit shocked. Me help a grown-up? Me solve a problem for Uncle John? I couldn't imagine such a thing, and I certainly never would have guessed in a million years that my uncle's problem had to do with his little brother, Bobby Riggs.

—⚋—

In 1973, Bobby Riggs was the top-ranking tennis player in the world in the fifty-five-to-fifty-nine-year-old division. This fact, alone, was probably enough to give him the confidence to challenge women's tennis champion and future Hall-of-Famer Billie Jean King and believe that he would be the victor, but it wasn't his only motive in calling for the match. The truth is that Bobby enjoyed being the center of attention, and, even more so, he liked to gamble, especially on himself. Fortunately for him, he had been pretty successful at it in the past. In fact, in 1939, Bobby bet that he would win all three Wimbledon titles (singles, doubles and mixed doubles) in London—a wager that served him very well when he became the only male tennis player in history to win all three in the same year. At the age of twenty-one, Bobby not only became the greatest tennis player in the world, but—because he was a betting man—he also became very rich.

He was an outstanding athlete and a larger-than-life character, but it was his challenge of Billie Jean King to a best-three-of-five-sets tennis match during the height of the women's liberation movement that cemented Bobby's place in history. The winner would not only secure bragging rights for his or her sex but would also walk away with what ultimately became $100,000.

At the time of Bobby's challenge, Billie Jean King was twenty-six years his senior. Then twenty-nine years old, she had recently led eight other female players, known as the "Original 9," in the establishment of a professional women's tennis circuit, which later came to be called the Women's Tennis Association. The tour's first name was "The Virginia Slims," named after the cigarette brand known at the time for its female-empowering slogan: "You've come a long way, baby." Not surprisingly for the era, the major sponsor was Philip Morris, the maker of Virginia Slims.

Despite the age difference, Billie Jean King was Bobby Riggs' female counterpart within the world of competitive tennis. She had won all the major women's championships many times over. She was *the* superstar of The Virginia Slims tour. She had recently been ranked as the number one female tennis player in the world (Though, she fell to second place shortly thereafter, when her nemesis, Margaret Court, reclaimed the top spot upon returning to competition after a maternity leave). Bobby had been the number one men's player in the world in 1939 and was still on top, in his age group, all these years later.

Bobby's confidence that he could beat Billie Jean, coupled with his fondness for gambling, caused him to make his initial $5,000 challenge. In 1973, five grand was a huge amount of money, a good deal more than Billie Jean could make winning a women's tournament. Sure, Bobby Riggs was a master gambler and an unapologetic self-promoter, but Billie Jean didn't exactly shy away from publicity. She constantly told reporters, fans—and anyone who would listen—that professional female tennis players were getting a raw deal: They were paid much less than their male counterparts. Establishing equal pay for equal play was one of the main reasons King helped to create The Virginia Slims series. This was the first time that pay inequality in tennis had been highlighted in a public way, and Billie Jean's fight soon became a cornerstone of the women's lib movement.

As Billie Jean's frequent doubles partner and fellow Original 9 member Rosie Casals once said, "We were fighting for our livelihood. We wanted to earn a living; we wanted to play sports; be accepted. People looked at us and said, 'Why aren't you in the kitchen? Why aren't you getting married, raising children?' We said, 'Why should we?'"

Bobby, however, didn't agree with the assertion that women should earn as much as men did, and he became the self-appointed spokesman against her campaign. He liked to point out that the "master men"—which included retired pros Pancho Segura, Pancho Gonzalez, and, of course, himself— played in tournaments that typically offered no prize money whatsoever. In fact, the players had to pay many of their own expenses. Always on the lookout for an opportunity to draw attention to himself and add fuel to the fire, Bobby injected his opinion into the argument. "Women athletes don't play as well as men, anyway," he said. "They're lucky to get paid as much as they do for their inferior performances. Even I, a relatively old man, could beat the best women tennis players in their prime."

But, he didn't stop there—Bobby Riggs knew an opportunity when he saw one, and this one was too good to pass up. So, he made a public declaration, stating that the master men could beat any woman pro, including the women's number one player. It was Billie Jean King that Bobby wanted to play because, among female athletes, she was the voice of women's liberation.

The Bobby-versus-Billie, male-versus-female feud was the most publicized sports battle at the time—and this was at the high point of the women's liberation movement. *The Mary Tyler Moore Show* was a huge hit, portraying Mary Richards as a successful TV producer (not a nurse or a teacher or a housewife) making a name for herself in a tough business without a husband by her side. Women marched and protested in the streets and burned their bras in public boycotts. Activist and author Betty Friedan said, "This is not a bedroom war. This is a political movement." Helen Reddy sang, "I Am Woman." The press ate up the prospect of a clash between the two outspoken tennis stars—the "Battle of the Sexes," as it would come to be known.

When I began my job as Bobby Riggs' scrapbook maker, I was aware of the feud, but only in a way that a kid could be aware of such things. A battle of the sexes sounded pretty interesting, but I didn't understand any of the background, politics or business behind the deal. And I knew almost nothing about the real characters of Bobby Riggs and Billie Jean King. To me, they were both loud and important stars.

However, I was more closely connected to Bobby Riggs than most people—kids or adults: My Aunt Marion, affectionately known as Auntie Bun, had married Bobby's older brother, my Uncle John Riggs. So, when I began putting together the scrapbooks in the spring of 1973, starting about six months before the match between Bobby and Billie Jean, I wasn't, by any means, a stranger to the man and his career.

Few remember the actual date, but most remember the match. You didn't have to follow tennis to hear about it— it was one of the most talked about and anticipated events in sports. The legendary Battle of the Sexes was held at the Houston Astrodome, the world's first domed sports stadium—known as the "eighth wonder of the world"—on Thursday, September 20, 1973. Billie Jean King had finally taken the great Bobby Riggs up on his offer, and as male faced female across the net, the world anxiously awaited the outcome. Could a woman actually beat a man in tennis, or in any sport? Were men really the dominant sex? Would Bobby Riggs hold on to his reputation as the greatest big-match tennis player in history, or would he lose it—and a bunch of money—to a woman?

I had a difficult time understanding the magnitude if this him-versus-her competition. After all, at my high school, we had only boys' sports teams. If you saw girls near the football field or on the basketball court, they were cheerleaders, not competitors.

In his typical style, it wasn't enough for Bobby to simply challenge Billie Jean. He was far too outspoken for that. The match gave him an opportunity to come out of retirement, monopolize the spotlight and boast about male superiority, particularly his, to every reporter who would listen.

Bobby loved to make outrageous statements, such as, "A woman's place is in the kitchen and the bedroom—and not necessarily in that order," and "A woman should be kept barefoot and pregnant." The battle was on!

His pregame bombast created a frenzy in the media. Bobby was in his element, taking full advantage of the opportunity to grant interviews and make the rounds on the talk-show circuit. Anyone who listened knew that his motivation for playing in the match had little to do with tennis and a whole lot to do with male chauvinism, as well as money.

Although I was young, Uncle John felt comfortable confiding in me his concerns about the impending showdown. "Billie Jean's been taking this seriously," he told me, on the flight from San Diego to Houston. "She's been training hard. Bobby hasn't been training at all. He's retired, but he has got to get ready for the match. He's gained ten pounds in the last four months. He hasn't played seriously or competitively for some time. He's spending all his time up at a playboy's mansion in Beverly Hills." Uncle John shook his head. "He's too busy shooting off his mouth to swing a racket." With the match approaching fast, Bobby should have been focusing on his game and getting back to his fighting weight, but that simply wasn't his style.

Because of the scrapbooks, nobody had to tell me that Bobby was spending most of his time promoting, rather than training for, the match. On a daily basis, I scanned fifteen to twenty newspapers, carefully clipped out any articles that mentioned Bobby, and organized them chronologically into letter-sized folders before affixing them to scrapbook pages. Each day, I read dozens of articles describing Bobby's promotional stunts in support of the Battle of the Sexes. One might have thought he was a spokesperson *for* the event, rather than a competitor in it.

In my opinion, his best promotional appearance took place on August 9, 1973, when he taught Johnny Carson how to play tennis on *The Tonight Show*. He and Johnny took turns hitting tennis balls into the curtain, and, at the end, the curtain opened, revealing a life-size cardboard cutout of Billie Jean King. Bobby jumped the net, placed a large bouquet of red roses in her arms and gave cardboard Billie Jean a kiss. It was the least he could do: After all, Billie Jean had returned him to center stage, a place he always wanted to be, and he was eating it up. Without a doubt, the episode was entertaining—Johnny was humorous, and Bobby was intense, as always. Outside of a few matches Bobby played to get his gambling fix, it was one of the few times he picked up a racket in the weeks before the Battle of the Sexes.

In addition to guest appearances on TV shows, the great huckster was busy doing television commercials. He sponsored Sugar Daddy caramel suckers, but his best TV ad, hands down, was for Hai Karate aftershave. The ad featured Bobby in a tennis dress, doing household chores, such as vacuuming and beating rugs on a clothesline (remember, washers and dryers were still a luxury in 1973). Then he turned to the camera, held up his bottle of Hai Karate and said, "After all, which would you rather be? A great women's tennis player, or a fifty-five-year-old sex symbol?" Then his "Bosom Buddies"—a troupe of sexy, scantily clad young women—ran out and surrounded him. During a press conference, he was quoted as saying, "I'm gonna wear Hai Karate aftershave so she'll think of me as a sex symbol, rather than a tennis opponent." Bobby wasn't shy about his beliefs— women belonged in the kitchen and in the bedroom, and not necessarily in that order.

It's been reported that Billie Jean turned down 2,000 offers for interviews, saying, "I'm going to let my racket speak for itself." Bobby, on the other hand, was so busy promoting the event and beefing up the hype that he didn't have any time left to train. According to Uncle John, the only body parts Bobby was exercising were his mouth and, well, another one I prefer not to mention.

Because I had just started my sophomore year at El Capitan High School in the small Southern California town of Lakeside, there were no plans for me to attend the Battle of the Sexes in Houston. Uncle John was going, and he'd purchased two plane tickets—one for himself and one for Auntie Bun.

However, Auntie Bun had always been a reluctant flyer, and it was going to take more than a tennis match to get her on an airplane. Plus, she'd never been fond of watching Bobby play; she'd seen him more times than she cared to count. Uncle John had tried to convince her to go this time, but she refused and wouldn't budge. So, at the last minute, I received a request to accompany my uncle to the biggest tennis match of my lifetime. Somehow, the powers that be agreed to let me go, even if it meant I had to miss almost a week of school.

I soon found out, though, that Uncle John had an ulterior motive for the invitation; he wanted me to gather material for the scrapbooks. But, the way he put it to me was, "Hey, as long as you're here, you might as well make yourself useful." We arrived two days before the match, and Uncle John told me to buy every newspaper, I could get my hands on, each day. He even handed me a bag of dimes to help get the job done. Admittedly, my task wasn't too difficult. For the most part, I could find the papers without having to search very far. All of the Houston newspapers were available at the hotel, as well as other major metropolitan papers, such as the *Los Angeles Times* and *The New York Times*, and virtually every one of them was giving extensive coverage to the events leading up to the match. Being the obedient scrapbook maker that I was, I scrambled to get the daily papers before they sold out. By the end of the week, they filled up an entire suitcase, which I took home with me to add to Bobby's scrapbooks.

While I could go on and on about the match, I won't. For one thing, the Battle of the Sexes is one of the most written-about sporting events in our country's history. I clipped and pasted thousands and thousands of articles on the topic. It was the subject of a made-for-television movie, *When Billie Beat Bobby*, starring Holly Hunter as Billie Jean. And forty years later, in 2013, I was involved as a consultant for *The Battle of the Sexes*, a documentary about the match. (This experience would prove to me once again the great value of my scrapbooking efforts, but I'll get to that later.)

Though I won't recount every detail of that day, I can give you a flavor of the battle, from the point of view of a by-then fifteen-year-old kid—well, at least as much as I could see, given my seat. It was a great spot, only two rows from the court, but unfortunately, George Foreman, the former heavyweight-boxing champion, and Jim Brown, the Hall of Fame running back and movie star, owned the seats in front of me. I'd never seen such wide shoulders in my life—and haven't since. While my view was significantly impeded by their broad physiques, the day wasn't a total loss. I was privileged to meet the lovely Blythe Danner, the 1970 Tony

Award winner for her performance in *Butterflies Are Free* and, to this day, my favorite actress. (She is also, of course, the mother of actress Gwyneth Paltrow and director Jake Paltrow.) That was the highlight of my trip, but I also saw Andy Williams and Farrah Fawcett in the crowd.

In lieu of the traditional player announcements, Bobby's voluptuous Bosom Buddies carried him out on a rickshaw, and the Rice University men's track team carried out Billie Jean on an Egyptian litter. Studying world history in high school at the time, I could only imagine that this scene was reminiscent of the battles of the Roman gladiators from centuries ago. Then, the presentations were made. Bobby gave Billie Jean a twenty-pound Sugar Daddy. Billie Jean presented Bobby with a baby pig, in recognition of the fact that he had proudly referred to himself as the "king of male chauvinist pigs." Billie Jean was wearing blue suede Adidas tennis shoes, and Bobby donned his Sugar Daddy jacket. The audience was both excited and divided. Many waved signs or wore shirts signifying which side they favored.

Bobby on a rickshaw carried in by the Bosom Buddies.

I had a difficult time rooting against Billie Jean because of my baseball addiction. I grew up a San Francisco Giants fan, and her baby brother, Randy Moffitt, pitched very capably for the team from 1972 to 1981. Still, I had a personal connection to Bobby, so I wanted him to do well.

The atmosphere was exactly as Bobby had intended it to be: Some referred to the event as a circus. But, Bobby wasn't the only one who had played a role in the enthusiasm. The promoter of the match was Jerry Perenchio, then best known for promoting the championship boxing match between Muhammad Ali and Joe Frazier in 1971. Perenchio was also Norman Lear's production partner in hugely successful television shows such as *All in the Family* and *Maude*. He later became the majority owner of the Spanish-language television network, Univision, and is rumored to be the most significant real estate owner in Malibu. His "Rules of the Road"—a set of twenty tenets by which he leads his life—starts with "Stay out of the spotlight, because it will fade your suit." One of the largest donors to the Republican Party in the United States' history, his net worth today is estimated to be $2.3 billion. Proving himself a marketing genius, Perenchio somehow managed to get the Houston Astrodome to pay him for the privilege of hosting the Battle of the Sexes.

The crowd of spectators that day amounted to 30,472 people, the largest ever for a tennis match up to that time, and, to this day, the second-largest live tennis audience in history. Some paid as much as $100 for their ticket to the match, which was a lot of money in the early 1970s. ABC got the rights to broadcast the event, and the worldwide television coverage was estimated to have attracted ninety million viewers. Howard Cosell was in the booth, along with female tennis pro Rosie Casals and retired men's pro Gene Scott. At the last minute, Scott had replaced Hall-of-Famer Jack Kramer, apparently at Billie Jean's demand, because Kramer had, in the past, made some very disparaging comments about women.

To me, it seemed more like a Broadway show than a sporting event. People weren't really interested in the tennis; they were interested in the spectacle. Expectations were high on both sides, and wagers were plenty. Before the match, Bobby was the favorite, with five-to-two odds. Leo Durocher, the badly behaved manager of the Houston Astros, was in Bobby's hotel room the afternoon before the tennis match. Like Bobby, Leo loved to gamble, and again like Bobby, he wagered heavily that Billie Jean King would lose.

Uncle John's premonition about Bobby failing to prove Billie Jean's sex the weaker one threatened to bear itself out in the warm-up. Bobby had several things going against him—he was fifty-five years old (Billie Jean was only twenty-nine), and he was retired and out of shape, while Billie Jean was at the top of her game, mentally and physically. During the week of the Battle of the Sexes, The Virginia Slims series was being held in Houston, and four days prior to her match with Bobby Riggs, Billie Jean had won her first- and second-round matches. There was no question that when she stepped onto the court for the Battle of the Sexes, she was in peak form.

Adding to Bobby's disadvantage was the Sugar Daddy jacket he insisted on wearing. While the Houston Astrodome was air-conditioned, the place was packed and very humid. Uncle John noticed the problem first, muttering, "Bobby needs to take off the damn jacket. He's already getting tired." But Bobby didn't. To my uncle's extreme distress, the "damn" jacket stayed on until Bobby trailed 2–1 in the first set. Finally, the jacket came off, but it was already too late. Bobby was sweating profusely. Uncle John was beside himself.

"This doesn't look good," Uncle John said. "I can't believe he left that damn jacket on for so long." Later, we found out why Bobby hadn't taken it off earlier. Apparently, Nabisco paid him a lot of money—I've heard $50,000 per year for the next ten years—to keep it on for a specific amount of time.

No, it didn't look good for Bobby Riggs. The air went out of his balloon: Billie Jean King hammered him in straight sets, 6–4, 6–3 and 6–3. The competition of all competitions wasn't much of a competition at all. At the match's conclusion, Billy Jean threw her racket high in the air. Bobby walked off the court and locked himself in the bathroom of his hotel room for four hours.

Billie Jean's dress is displayed next to Bobby's Sugar Daddy jacket from "Battle of the Sexes".

Chapter 3

"Your Auntie Bun Is Going to Divorce Me."

"What problem are you talking about?" I asked Uncle John, continuing the most fateful conversation of my young life.

"Scrapbooks," he said. "I've got a problem with Bobby Riggs' scrapbooks. Your Auntie Bun is going to divorce me if I don't get them done."

Scrapbooks? Divorce? Uncle John was speaking to me like an adult, something I had rarely experienced. And the gravity of what he had to say made me nervous.

—⁓—

If it hadn't been for this phone call, that spring day—and maybe even the entirety of 1973—would have been forgettable. Instead, I got involved with the Bobby Riggs legacy and would later get my chance to witness the Battle of the Sexes, the most publicized event—but probably also the least meaningful—I learned about, as I put the scrapbooks together. The match was a bust as far as drama goes, and a bust in terms of what it has meant to me in the years since I sat clipping articles. The real value of putting together those scrapbooks wouldn't reveal itself for decades.

I was just fourteen when I got the scrapbooking gig, and I was living a relatively uneventful life. I was like other kids my age; school and homework consumed most of my time. I was very studious, having achieved straight A's in junior high, and I played point guard on the boys' freshman basketball team—these two activities kept me really busy. One day blended into another, until the days, weeks and months all blurred into one, forming what I'd someday remember as my youth. But, one phone call changed all of that.

"Auntie Bun" was the nickname given to Marion Riggs, my father's only sibling. That made her husband, John Riggs, my uncle by marriage. In addition to his booming voice, Uncle John also had numerous brothers—the youngest of which was the famous Bobby Riggs.

At the time, Uncle John and Auntie Bun resided in Coronado, about a thirty-minute drive from our house. We lived in Lakeside, Calif., a small town in San Diego's East

County, where my father was superintendent of Lakeside Elementary School District. I was the youngest son of Dr. Robert Muscio and Dolores Muscio, and everyone called me "Dick." In the early spring of 1973, I was nearing the final stretch of my freshman year at El Capitan High School, where my older brother, Bob, was a sophomore.

When Uncle John asked for my help, I was already aware that Bobby was up to something—something big. About a month earlier, I had accompanied Uncle John to a press conference at the ritzy Westgate Hotel in downtown San Diego. There, Bobby put on a grand show in front of a room packed with newspaper and TV reporters and white-gloved waiters. Waving a $5,000 cashier's check in the air, Bobby shouted out (in a manner of speaking, as Bobby's voice could best be described as squeaky) a challenge to the best women's tennis player on the planet. To the tune of five grand, he issued a public wager to Billie Jean King, claiming that even he—a middle-aged man—could beat her. The ball, so to speak, was now in her court.

At last, Uncle John got to his primary question, "Do you know how to make scrapbooks?"

I had never made a scrapbook in my life. I had never even seen one. I had no idea what it involved, but I thought it would be cool to get my first job and to document the achievements of the man who was, in my mind, the world's greatest tennis player.

So I lied and said yes. With that one word, I became Bobby Riggs' scrapbook maker.

A few weeks later, on Easter Sunday, my family drove to Coronado to spend the afternoon with Auntie Bun and Uncle John. It was my first glimpse into the monumental project I had taken on. Uncle John hadn't been exaggerating when he said it was no small job—there were so many piles of magazines and newspapers that we could barely walk into the den. As I looked at the stacks and stacks of documents and materials, I could understand the urgency behind Uncle John's call—after all, Auntie Bun was a neat freak and Uncle John…well, let's just say he was a procrastinator. I could just imagine the ultimatum she'd handed him before he placed the call, now that I was finally witnessing the sheer size of the problem. In fact, I'm surprised she hadn't delivered one long before—that's how massive the piles of newspapers and magazines were.

Together, we all dove in, carrying piles of paper and material down to my father's car. If there had been one more load, we wouldn't have been able to close the trunk. When we were done, my Auntie Bun was overjoyed; her den was clean. And Uncle John was relieved; his burden had been lifted. I was happy, and so were my parents—after all, I had just gotten my very first job. And it wasn't just any job—I was about to become a scrapbook maker for a famous tennis player.

My life changed in the following months. Scrapbooks now took up the time that had once been consumed by homework. From Easter 1973 to January of 1974, I spent all my time outside of school working on them. The articles came nonstop, from all over the United States, as well as from other countries. Bobby didn't personally send me the articles—he subscribed to clipping services, and they were the ones charged with the responsibility of finding articles that mentioned his name. Actually, the term *clipping service* is quite a misnomer, considering the fact that these services never actually clipped anything. Instead, they sent the entire magazine or newspaper, leaving me with the daunting task of searching for the article inside that mentioned Bobby Riggs. Early on, I found that newspapers were the easiest to work with—Bobby's name was usually found in the sports section. In magazines, though, it was a bit more challenging. I'd have to read the entire thing from cover to cover to make sure I didn't miss anything. Fortunately for me, I liked to read.

In addition to handling the steady stream of new periodicals stuffed into our mailbox every day, I also had to tackle the task of completing the scrapbooks started by Ruth Wells, Bobby's former lover. Using a manual typewriter, I set out to create an index of each scrapbook, going page by page and listing the title of the article, the name of the magazine or newspaper, and the date of publication. It was a tedious undertaking—each scrapbook contained more than 200 pages, and each index averaged about twenty pages.

In the process, I noticed that Ruth had credited herself for preparing the scrapbooks by affixing a small "prepared by" placard to each one. While I acknowledged her contribution, I also gave myself due recognition by adding another placard crediting myself for the indices. When I was done finishing up the old books, I felt a sense of relief and accomplishment. Having tidied up Ruth's work, I could now turn my attention to preparing new scrapbooks to hold the content we'd received from Uncle John and the abundance of material that was arriving by mail on a daily basis, much to our rural postman's chagrin.

I had always perceived Ruth to be a helpful and kind person, so when I had a question about the project, I was comfortable reaching out to her. As I began my first scrapbook, I knew I had to do it right and make sure it matched the ones she had made.

Contents of Book 10

An example of the catalog of contents contained in book 10.

BOOK 10 PREPARED BY

AND CONTENTS TYPED BY

DICK MUSCIO

1975 - 1976

Cover plate of scrapbook #10.

These scrapbooks were much larger compared to the standard eight-and-a-half-by-eleven size, and the outside covers were shiny and colorful, with vibrant shades of orange, blue and purple. Ruth came through for me, letting me know that she had purchased her scrapbooks at Warwick's in La Jolla. So, my mom drove me to Warwick's, where we bought more scrapbooks, lots of thick paper to fill them with, and glue and sundry supplies. Fully stocked, I was ready to get back to work.

I took my job seriously, knowing that if I slacked off, even just a little, I would never be able to keep up with the increasing number of articles that were piling up in my room. So, I developed a system: I'd clip each article and its heading from the periodical in question and then place each one, in order by date, in a letter-sized file. Next, I would glue each article into the scrapbook, careful to keep them in chronological order. When a scrapbook could no longer hold any more pages, I would pull out the manual typewriter and meticulously type the completed book's index. The finishing step came when I affixed a small placard to the left inside cover crediting "Dick Muscio" with the making of the scrapbook, as well as the creation of the chronological index. That was my crowning moment in the first ten scrapbooks, but because I had school commitments and time constraints, my mom finished the last one, so the eleventh and final scrapbook was credited to "Dolores Muscio," and rightfully so.

I found that making scrapbooks was very time consuming, especially when you were documenting a high-profile athlete such as Bobby Riggs. On top of the sheer volume of content, the gluing and drying process slowed me down, too. I learned that when I glued an article to the front of a page and then turned it over and immediately glued another to the reverse, I'd create a mess. The glue simply had to dry on one side before I could move on to the other. So, I used my enjoyment of reading to fill the optimal two-minute gap. I read—a lot. I read about Bobby's career and the outrageous quotes he spouted. I also read about sports, in general, sports of every kind, in every major city. But I didn't limit myself to that—I became knowledgeable about many other important matters, including the end of the Vietnam War, the start of Watergate, Roe v. Wade, women's liberation and our country's first OPEC oil embargo experience. I wasn't just any scrapbook maker—I was a supremely well-informed one.

I was also a glue sniffer. I sniffed glue all spring, summer, and fall that year—not because I was trying to get high but because it was a part of the trade. I sniffed, I read and I typed—and I got pretty good at all three.

I might not remember much about 1972 or 1974, but ask me anything about 1973 and I'll be all over it. Though slated to be an uneventful year, 1973 became one that I'll never forget. It was the year I got my first job and became a connoisseur of the news. It was the year I documented the career achievements of the world's greatest tennis player. It was also the year that I single-handedly saved a marriage.

This project, combined with my academic responsibilities, consumed my daily life. I didn't go out on a single date in 1973, nor did I attend prom. I did not attend a single Friday night football game during the fall of 1973. After playing basketball on the freshman team in the fall of 1972, I didn't have time to play on the junior varsity basketball team when the season started up the next year. But that's what happens when you spend almost one thousand hours creating about 2,500 pages of oversized scrapbook material and more than 200 pages of chronological indices, all meticulously typed— with no errors—on a manual typewriter.

Chapter 4

Bobby Riggs, the Champion

"*I* promised Bobby I would get his scrapbooks done, but I haven't even started," Uncle John told me on the day he called to recruit me. "I can't believe I told him yes, but I did, so now I've just got to get this done." There was a tone in his voice I hadn't heard before. He sounded like one of my friends who hadn't done his homework.

Ahhh, so that's what this was about. He didn't need me to stop an impending divorce, after all. No, he just needed me to step in and save him from the wrath Auntie Bun was sure to unleash if he let his brother Bobby down.

"So, can you give me a hand?"

—⁓—

Before I answered Uncle John, I tested his patience by asking him a few questions. His replies provided some background into the scrapbooks, and a lot more.

By building the scrapbooks, I learned a lot more about Bobby Riggs than just the details of his match with Billie Jean King. In many ways, the Billie Jean story was one of the less interesting events in Bobby's career.

As my scrapbooking efforts would teach me, Bobby was undoubtedly one of the greatest tennis players of the twentieth century. Born on February 25, 1918, in Los Angeles, the last of six siblings born to a Pentecostal minister, Bobby proved himself to be an outstanding athlete at an early age; first as a table-tennis player and then as a tennis player after he took up the latter sport at age eleven. In the years before big-money sports, when tennis development programs didn't exist, Bobby learned the game by playing on public courts in Los Angeles. By age eighteen, he was the Southern California men's titleholder and ranked number four in the United States.

Standing only five feet seven inches, he was small. His tennis game lacked power, but he possessed brains, foot speed and incredible ball control. He rose to a number-one world ranking in 1939, when he won the US Open, and was the only player in history to win Wimbledon singles, doubles and mixed doubles in the same year (it was during that tournament that he'd made a small fortune betting on himself).

He won the US Open again in 1941; however, his career was then interrupted by military service with the Navy. Bobby did not serve in active duty, but he spent the war entertaining troops at military bases with tennis and table-tennis exhibitions. He was assigned to the US Navy Athletic Special Services Division under the direction of heavyweight-boxing champion Gene Tunney, and, during his naval tour, he played tennis against US Vice President Henry Wallace and Vice Admiral John Hoover, among many others.

A younger Bobby Riggs

Bobby returned to tennis as a pro after World War II because he needed to make money, and he won the US Pro Championships in 1946, 1947 and 1949. Recall, however, that many great players still retained amateur status at this time, as the prospect of steady income as a "teaching pro" was a safer bet for most, rather than going out on pro tours in the days before television brought huge cash prizes into the equation. This watered down Bobby's competition somewhat. His two main antagonists were fellow future Hall-of-Famers Don Budge and Jack Kramer, both much harder hitters of the ball.

As his professional career wound down in his early thirties, Bobby began promoting tennis events as a way of making money in the sport without playing. I didn't really know what a promoter was until I started reading about Bobby, and it took me a while to figure out what exactly he did. This business primarily consisted of traveling exhibition tours with Jack Kramer and Pancho Gonzalez, as well as promoting "Gorgeous Gussie" Moran, the first women's tennis sex symbol.

Gussie Moran was a long-legged twenty-six-year-old bombshell from Santa Monica, Calif., who was not without some skill in the sport. She rose as high as number four in the world, at one point in her career. Bobby bet that her great looks and daring wardrobe (designed by Teddy Tinling, the fashion designer who, twenty years later, would create the dress Billie Jean King wore at the Battle of the Sexes) would draw spectators to his exhibition tours, and he was right.

But, Bobby ran into trouble when he started promoting other sporting events. That stage of his career was derailed by a failed baseball postseason barnstorming tour; horrific winter weather and Bobby's lack of attention to detail turned the tour into a flop.

Bobby's personal life was as turbulent as his tennis career. Since my family life was so stable, this was also an eye-opener for me. After divorcing his first wife, Kay Fischer, in 1952 after thirteen years of marriage, Bobby married Priscilla Wheelan in the same year. He also moved into corporate life with a position as executive vice president and then president of American Photograph Corporation in New York. The business was owned by Priscilla's father, R. B. Wheelan, and was hugely successful as a student photography company for schools. Bobby, however, was not happy as a corporate executive, even though he needed the income of a steady job. He couldn't help being who he was—a competitor and a risk taker. Thus, Bobby spent considerable time "chasing the action" on the golf course and continued competing in age-group tennis events ("the masters"). Bobby was simply not wired to sit behind a desk. This was no doubt part of his motivation for getting back into the limelight with the Battle of the Sexes.

After fathering two children with his first wife, Kay (Robert Jr. and Larry), he had three children with Priscilla (James, Billy and Dorothy a.k.a. Dolly). He also became the legal father of John, whom Priscilla had from her previous marriage. In 1967, Bobby was elected to the tennis Hall of Fame.

As I was putting the scrapbooks together, it was difficult for me to build the articles into the portrait of a man. I didn't understand what life was all about, much less what the life of a gambling sports star like Bobby Riggs was all about. Back then, sports was all about "the thrill of victory and the agony of defeat," at least, according to ABC's popular show *The Wide World of Sports*. Commentators focused on the performance, not the lives of athletes. And, very few athletes made a lot of money back then. Bobby broke the mold in many ways, and I sat there with the scrapbooks trying to figure it all out.

I have asserted that Bobby said outrageous things about women not out of malice but in order to garner publicity and make money, but it is true that he was a philandering husband and an absentee father, especially to his two children with Kay (Robert Jr. and Larry), and he had strained relationships with Billy and his daughter, Dolly. This was evidenced by his son Larry's frequent extended stays at my Auntie Bun and Uncle John's Sacramento home, prior to their move to Southern California in 1969.

None of Bobby's children measured up to their father athletically—Larry came the closest as an excellent tennis player and, later, a collegiate tennis coach—but, unless his kids wanted to play sports and watch sports, it was hard for Bobby to find time for them. Further, when he played tennis or table tennis with them, he did not coddle them. He competed fiercely with his children, as he did in every game. This, no doubt, exacerbated the strained relationships.

Priscilla's alcoholism—which I, of course, didn't know about as a kid—added to the marital strife. Perhaps one of the reasons Bobby needed to get back in the spotlight and "chase the action" was to escape his troubled marriage. Journalist Jon Bradshaw once wrote that, when Bobby—now a deskbound corporate executive—walked into a bar or a party, not a single person knew who he was. Bobby couldn't stand this, which is probably the main reason he kept trying to get back in the limelight.

In addition to craving attention, Bobby was also a gambling addict. I'd guess that there's no truth to the rumor that his first words, at the tender age of one, were "Wanna bet?" This was a guess based on the ironic fact that Bobby was the last child of Gideon Riggs, a very strict Pentecostal minister. At the time of Bobby's birth, Gideon was fifty years old and was recognized in Los Angeles as a very serious and successful ambassador for his church. Thus, I suspect that "Wanna bet?" came shortly after "Yes, sir" and "No, ma'am."

Bobby was once reported to say, "When I wake up in the morning, if there isn't something big to bet on and play in, then I find something small to bet on and play in. And, if there isn't something small, then I stay in bed." Bobby never stayed in bed, and Bobby never considered himself a gambling addict, because addicts were losers and he was a winner. He had proven as much at Wimbledon in 1939. On the golf course, according to my Uncle John, Bobby hung around with guys who had such nicknames as Charlie the Blade, Three-Iron Ward and Shaggy Ralph.

Bobby divorced Priscilla in 1972 and reemerged as a swinging bachelor just before the Battle of the Sexes, wearing a toupée to mask early balding. Bobby made history of sorts in the divorce proceedings, insofar as it was *he* who received a significant financial settlement—rumored to be one million dollars—from her. As he promoted the Battle of the Sexes, Bobby liked to say that he was a "retired millionaire." He never mentioned the source of his wealth, for obvious reasons.

Still, family meant something to Bobby. He enjoyed spending time with his brother, my Uncle John, and every now and then, they'd let me come along for the ride. Once, as the three of us were hitting golf balls at a driving range, Bobby took a practice swing and accidentally nicked me in the forehead. I was about 11, and had been standing right behind him. I traded a little bit of blood for all the ice cream I could eat, and Bobby was profusely apologetic.

In the spring of 1976, Bobby and Priscilla's twenty-two-year-old son James died of an apparent drug overdose. Shortly thereafter, Bobby remarried Priscilla, and the couple remained together until Priscilla passed away in early 1995.

Bobby's self-centeredness and flamboyant public persona is evidenced by a couple of lapel pins included in the scrapbooks. Produced for his post-Battle of the Sexes touring days, the pins read "I was hustled by Bobby Riggs" and "Bobby Riggs likes girls." Bobby was also very tight with money, except in cases when someone had done great favors for him; then, he was sometimes quite generous, especially with my Uncle John. He made sure his older brother always had lots of cash.

However, I still don't understand, and somewhat resent, how Bobby treated my cousin, Frances. Frances assisted him and Priscilla greatly as their caretaker in their later years, yet he left her no money in his will. Frances had a difficult life, both health-wise and financially, and her monetary needs were ultimately taken care of thanks to Auntie Bun and Uncle John's will and my attention and care as her cousin and trustee. This is one instance in which Bobby's mercurial nature and pathological egomania impacted me personally, and it was one of the reasons I would later devote my life to building a caring and tolerant community.

Looking back on what I learned from making the scrapbooks in 1973, I am amazed at the misconceptions promoted by the press. Many people in the press reported that Bobby couldn't possibly really be like his public persona. Well, if you have any doubts, go back and read this chapter one more time. I assure you, the great champion was Bobby 24/7. There was no "public" and "private" persona—Bobby wasn't a man of pretense, and he didn't put on airs in public. He was unapologetically himself, at all times.

Besides Kay, Priscilla and Billie Jean, one other woman played a key role in Bobby's strange journey. She was, perhaps, the most important of them all.

Chapter 5

The Mother's Day Massacre

"Bobby has broken up with Ruth," Uncle John explained as he described the scrapbook project to me. "Now, that he's back in the spotlight, he's hanging around with all of these blondes who get paid by sponsors to show up at his promotional events."

—m—

Although Ruth, who lived nearby, in La Jolla, had been known as "Bobby's mistress," I didn't find the term *mistress* very fitting. To me, a mistress was a secret—someone kept behind closed doors. In our family, Ruth wasn't a secret—she was well liked, and I always found her warm, intelligent and engaging. I suspect she was a major reason behind Bobby's divorce from Priscilla, but as a fourteen-year old, I didn't spend time thinking about such things. Ruth was the one who'd started making the scrapbooks, and when she and

Bobby broke up in early 1973, she abandoned the project, turning the books over to my Uncle John. Recently retired from his career as a criminal investigator for the state of California, Uncle John had some free time, so he promised his brother that he could take it on.

I also learned that while both Ruth and Uncle John had good intentions, the scrapbooks were missing some important parts. Nobody had prepared an index or chronology of the articles, and a significant amount of content had yet to be inserted. But that wasn't all—according to Uncle John, Bobby was destined to increase his stardom, which would mean a significant increase in the publicity he'd receive for the rest of the year. Sheepishly, Uncle John admitted that this scrapbook project was more than he could handle.

I could barely believe what I was hearing over the phone. Uncle John was opening his heart to me in a way he never had before. It was mysterious and thrilling to be given this insight into the world of adults. I sensed that the scrapbooks would open up a whole new world for me. In retrospect, that reason was a huge part of why I said yes.

I will forever assert that the tennis match between Margaret Court and Bobby Riggs on Mother's Day in 1973— May 13, to be exact—is the most important tennis match played in the history of the United States, even though it's one that nobody seems to remember...except me.

At the time it took place, I was knee-deep in the scrapbooks and knew every detail ever printed about Bobby. To this day, I can recite the details of the match from memory. I had the good fortune of being there in person, at the San Vicente Country Club on the grounds of San Diego Country Estates, outside the small East County town of Ramona, not far from my home.

Why does hardly anyone remember this tennis match? Well, there are many reasons, but the most obvious is that, 130 days later, the Battle of the Sexes at the Houston Astrodome so overshadowed and outpaced Court vs. Riggs that most forgot, if they ever knew, where the journey started. To compound matters, the earlier match took place somewhere beyond the middle of nowhere. While my hometown of Lakeside was remote and rural, Ramona was even further off of the proverbial beaten path. Regardless of its nearly forgotten place in history, I believe that the 1973 Mother's Day Massacre—and the role it played in the Battle of the Sexes—requires some explanation.

At first, Billie Jean King had resisted Bobby's frequent challenges to a match. Bobby had focused on playing her because she was just as vocal in defending women's tennis and decrying pay inequality in the sport as he was in claiming that he, at the age of fifty-five, could beat any female player on the planet. In the early 1970s, male professional players made five to ten times more money than their female counterparts. Righting this wrong had become Billie Jean King's mission, as evidenced by her leadership role within the Original 9 and her part in the formation of The Virginia Slims tour.

Margaret Court, on the other hand, seemed to care very little about women's liberation. She was never heard championing this cause, and she had no interest in being one of the Original 9 (she was not) or in playing in the inaugural Virginia Slims series (she did not). But like Billie Jean, Margaret was not making very much money playing tennis, even though she had stepped back over Billie Jean and up to the top ranking in 1973. While it was clearly Billie Jean King that Bobby hoped to play, her refusal opened the door for him to consider Margaret as the second-best choice.

Born in a remote part of Australia, Margaret Smith Court was tall, strong, happily married (as she remains to this day), a mother and aloof. Elected to the tennis Hall of Fame in 1979, she dominated her counterparts with arguably the best serve-and-volley game in the history of women's tennis—at least, when she wasn't taking time off to have babies. Winner of more Grand Slam singles championships (24) than any other player in history—male or female, past or present—she was a dominating presence on the tour.

Margaret was also very conservative. She, in fact, disagreed with Billie Jean's push to create a separate tour for the women, reasoning that the absence of men would cause the women players to become inclined to experiment with homosexuality. "I thought it represented a moral slide," Margaret said. "I thought it was healthier for the men and the women to be together."

Margaret negotiated Bobby's initial $5,000 challenge, which Billie Jean had unceremoniously rejected, up to $10,000, and the date was set. Bobby called it "the Match of the Century," and some others called it "the Battle of the Sexes," but neither name stuck.

Next was the issue of where to hold the contest. Margaret lobbied for a Florida venue, but Bobby insisted on the brand-spanking-new San Vicente Country Club, where a good friend of Bobby's—former tennis professional Tony Trabert— had been named director of tennis operations. The business enterprise behind the country club was a very ambitious real estate development owned by the Watt Companies (founded by the legendary Southern California developer Ray Watt). The development consisted of more than 3,000 vacant lots, as well as one of the first large-scale timeshare programs in the history of the United States.

Mr. Watt was, like Bobby, a master self-promoter. He sought to host this tennis event at his new club in the hope that he could convince the Hollywood set to trek south 120 miles, where he would entice them to buy from his inventory of vacant lots, on which they would hopefully build many glorious vacation homes. (Bobby Riggs would later end up buying a vacation home in the development.)

The San Diego County Board of Supervisors had passed Mr. Watt's development plans by only a 3–2 vote. Little did they know their decision would play such an important role in the history of women's liberation. Watt lobbied hard to host the event at his country club, and Margaret eventually gave in.

I couldn't have been more excited about the location had it been in my own backyard. Ramona was in close proximity to my home, just northeast of the small town of Lakeside. I would venture a guess that, if you were to look up "small town" in the dictionary, it would show a picture of Lakeside. Compared to Ramona and its suburb of San Vicente, Lakeside seemed like a bustling metropolis. To get from Lakeside to San Vicente, at that time, required a twenty-mile drive through the middle of nowhere; eventually, you arrived at the far eastern fringe of nowhere. While Mr. Watt was ultimately successful with his timeshare development, San Vicente is quite remote, even today.

Certainly, this was the biggest sporting event to ever hit our rather dusty backwater of a region, and it created a great deal of excitement among many Lakeside residents, including me. Not only was I given the responsibility of making scrapbooks that contained every piece of news about the upcoming match, but I was also going to get to attend it in person with my family (this did not please my mother— attending one of Bobby Riggs's tennis matches was hardly her first choice of activities on Mother's Day).

Bobby Riggs took the match with Margaret Court very seriously, in sharp contrast to how he would later approach his battle with Billie Jean. He practiced regularly with his tennis partner, Lorne Kuhle. (At the time, Kuhle was twenty-nine years old; today, he is the proprietor of the Bobby Riggs Tennis Club in Encinitas, Calif., and the curator of the Bobby Riggs Tennis Museum, which is set on the club's grounds.) Bobby even set up shop at the villas at San Vicente and religiously ran at least one mile on the golf course every day. He also hired a nutritionist and starting consuming between 60 and 200 vitamins and supplements a day (the exact number depends on whose story you believe). At one point, Bobby said he had to have a glass stomach to be taking so many pills. By the time of the Battle of the Sexes, the pills were the only part of the training regimen that Bobby still followed.

While Bobby was getting in shape, so was the San Vicente Country Club. The match was to be played on court number one. Cement stands were already in place between the villas and the court, and temporary bleachers were set up on adjacent court number two. Total seating has been estimated between 3,500 and 5,000, but I believe the lesser number is more accurate. The television audience would watch the match on CBS, and the network had set up its cameras on the south end of the court. I was busy finding, reading, clipping and gluing the many articles published leading up to the event. Bobby, the tennis club and court, and the scrapbooks were all rounding into shape at the same time.

Margaret Court did not arrive until Friday, May 11, only two days before the match. She brought her husband and their one-year-old son, Danny, and the family took up residence at the villas, just down the hall from her opponent's room. I can only imagine what went through Margaret's mind as her family made the trip, driving from San Diego's airport and its very cosmopolitan downtown; heading east, past the entrance to my high school, El Capitan; then winding through the barren Barona Indian Reservation (which, today has a very vibrant casino and hotel) and its wide-open spaces on which horses and cattle grazed; and then moving on to the sagebrush beyond the reservation and the almost vacant San Vicente valley, through which both drugs and illegal aliens were smuggled from Mexico.

Margaret grew up in a very small and isolated town in Australia, so she would have been familiar with desolate countryside. However, considering she was about to play a tennis match of such magnitude, this remote setting must have seemed quite unsettling. And, it surely added to Margaret's potential unease when her baby dropped one of her tennis shoes in the toilet on the morning of the match.

True to form, Bobby Riggs never stopped talking in the days leading up to the match, telling anyone who cared to listen—as well as many who didn't—that this was the biggest match in tennis history. He also asserted that he was the best big-match player in the history of tennis. Modesty wasn't one of Bobby's attributes, and, at times like these, he was the epitome of cockiness. Still, he gave Margaret some credit, acknowledging that she was young and fast and strong. However, on the heels of the compliment, he also stated that she "hit the tennis ball like a man" and was "money hungry."

Leading up to the match, Margaret practiced with the club's director of tennis operations, Tony Trabert. Tony still hit the ball pretty hard—as hard as you would expect a former professional men's tennis player to hit. But, Bobby didn't hit the ball the way Tony did: Bobby preferred spins and lobs and slices and angles. This mismatch might have been lost on Margaret, and certainly the man-versus-woman hype didn't concern her. Margaret confirmed as much, stating that the "women's lib thing" wasn't something she cared about or followed. She was there for only one reason—to play tennis.

Driving from up the hill from Lakeside to San Vicente for the early afternoon match, we had to turn on the windshield wipers, not because it was raining, but because we drove smack-dab through the middle of a cloud. We used our wipers again on the way home, but the match was spared from the elements that day. Fortune smiled upon the San Vicente valley: the clouds lifted and the sun shone for the entirety of the match, but as soon as it ended, the cloud cover set in once again.

Pat Summerall served as the announcer for the CBS telecast, which was estimated to have at least ten million viewers. Among those attending the event was actor John Wayne, who also presented the winner's check to the victor. Bobby's manager, Jackie Barnett, best known for being Jimmy Durante's manager, was there as well. We sat in the third row, behind the area where the combatants sat during game changeovers.

The grand entrance was more subdued than that of the Battles of the Sexes. Before the match began, Bobby handed Margaret a dozen red roses—after all, it was Mother's Day, and Margaret was a relatively new mother. Accepting the bouquet before a full house, the Australian champion curtsied in appreciation. The stands and bleachers were full, with a few onlookers standing on the hill above the court. Many of the female attendees showed their support by wearing lapel pins that read "Women's libbers speak for themselves... Bobby Riggs—Bleah!" Margaret had even pinned one on her one-year-old son's bib.

Because Ray Watt's ulterior motive was to attract celebrities and sell timeshares and vacant lots, he donated the proceeds from ticket sales for the event to the San Diego County Diabetes Association. This move was rather admirable, considering that Mr. Watt's expenses for hosting the event were estimated to be as much as $30,000. Yet, he knew that the value of the coverage was worth millions of dollars.

Ticket used for admission to the Riggs vs. Court match.

There certainly was a lot of money at stake—for Mr. Watt, the media, and the players, who, let's not forget, were vying for a $10,000 check. Given all the publicity and money involved, CBS must have been disappointed when they were faced with dead airtime after it was over. The match lasted less than one hour—in two sets, Bobby Riggs annihilated Margaret Court,

6–2 and 6–1. Bobby dominated the court, hitting spins, dinks and lobs. Margaret self-destructed, making many crucial errors. Fewer than half of her first serves were served in. Bobby—probably grandstanding—even hit one of his serves underhanded, but Margaret sent it whistling back for a clean winner (one of her few).

Bobby had done his fair share of talking before the match, and he wasn't about to stop once he'd secured a victory. In his opinion, this had been the biggest event in tennis history, and he was "prepared" and "ready to answer the bell." Bobby proclaimed himself "the best big-game player ever." He boasted that he had proven his ability to beat any female tennis player—even though he'd beaten just one.

Margaret couldn't argue that she'd lost, but she didn't agree that it had anything to do with gender. "I didn't even think about the women's lib thing," she stated, before adding that perhaps she should have practiced against someone "who didn't hit the ball very hard and used a lot of spins." Famous for her serve-and-volley game, Margaret concluded by saying she could never play aggressively because when she tried to, she "couldn't hit the ball where she wanted to." Margaret still doesn't like to talk about the Mother's Day Massacre. Looking back many years later, she said simply, "It was one of my mistakes."

"Bobby Riggs Bleah!"
pin worn by fans.

Margaret post-match.

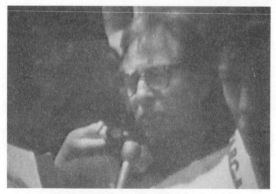

Bobby being interviewed after the match.

In his post-match interviews, Bobby said, "Now I want King bad. I'll play her on clay, grass, wood, cement, marble or roller skates." He added, "We got to keep this sex thing going. I'm a woman specialist now. I want her [King]. She's the women's libber leader."

The cover of the following week's *Sports Illustrated*, dated May 21, 1973, had featured Bobby under the heading, "Never Bet Against This Man." The article was titled "Mother's Day Ms. Match," a moniker I wish would have won out over "Mother's Day Massacre."

Margaret Court is now a very successful minister and television-show host in Australia. Her program is fundamentalist Christian and, not surprisingly, very conservative. She sometimes uses her platform to speak out against gay rights in Australia. Because of her conservative nature, her reluctance to become involved in equal rights or the women's liberation movement, and her views on homosexuality, I suspect that Margaret prays for Billie Jean King's soul from time to time. As their beliefs are concerned, the two women are at opposite ends of the spectrum. Despite Margaret's record number of Grand Slam singles titles, she was first and foremost a wife, a mother and a Christian. Furthermore, the women's liberation movement had started in the United States, and Australian Margaret wasn't attuned to the same cultural shifts as Americans were. Margaret and Billie Jean were worlds apart, in more ways than one.

The Mother's Day Massacre was a historic and monumental event. Unfortunately, the Battle of the Sexes got far more media coverage. One reason why many don't remember the first match is that it took place on Mother's Day—undoubtedly, many potential viewers had other plans. As a result, some watched only part of the match, and some didn't watch it at all. Also, I suspect that Bobby's first set 6–2 win caused many viewers to turn off the broadcast. After all, who wants to watch a train wreck in slow motion on Mother's Day? Even if it had been a different day, I'm relatively certain a lot of people would have lost interest and switched the channel after it became apparent that Margaret would lose. Finally, there were, at most, 4,000 people in attendance, and if statistical probabilities apply, given how many years it has been since the match took place, I doubt if there are even 1,500 people left on this planet who were there. Billie Jean King, who wasn't there, acknowledges that she didn't watch the match on television.

At one of her recent presentations, Billie Jean was asked by an audience member, "At what moment in time do you think Margaret lost the match?" Billie Jean's reply was telling: "When Bobby gave her the roses and she curtsied. Margaret never should have curtsied." Billie Jean also made this point: Margaret's resistance to female empowerment made her incapable of understanding the magnitude of what she had gotten herself into when she agreed to play Bobby. He was a great tennis player, but he was an even better hustler, and he'd succeeded in hustling the number one women's player in the world. In the post-match interview, Margaret was beyond disconsolate. That footage is hard to watch, even for a Bobby Riggs booster like me. Yet, I admit I've watched it many, many times.

So what does any of this have to do with the Battle of the Sexes? What role did the events before, during and after the Mother's Day Massacre have in convincing Billie Jean to finally take Bobby up on his challenge? In my opinion, their role was pivotal. I assert that the Battle of the Sexes would never have taken place if it hadn't been for the fact that Margaret Court lost on that fateful day. Even though she claimed that the match had nothing to do with advancing the women's movement, I beg to differ.

It's a given that the person Bobby really wanted to compete against was Billie Jean—primarily because she was not shy about asserting that female tennis players should be entitled to the same pay as men. The challenge he presented to her was more personal than professional. Had it been purely professional, had Billie Jean not been an outspoken promoter of women's rights, it's highly unlikely that Bobby would've shown any particular interest in the match. He certainly wouldn't have been so persistent in provoking her to accept his offer.

But, why does it matter whether he played Billie Jean or Margaret first? Remember, in 1973, Margaret had retaken the number one ranking, one spot ahead of Billie Jean. Also, in lifetime head-to-head matches, Margaret had defeated Billie Jean either 22–10 (per Bud Collins) or 21–13 (per Wikipedia), but, in either instance, Margaret "had Billie Jean's number." This head-to-head record, revealing Margaret to be the superior player, makes Billie Jean's eventual conquest of Bobby even more significant. In a sense, it nullified his previous victory over Margaret.

I propose that the Battle of the Sexes would have never been played if Margaret Court had defeated Bobby on Mother's Day in 1973. Had this happened, there would've been no point in holding a second match, Margaret would have proven that Bobby wasn't the greatest big-match tennis player in the world, and more important, would have confirmed that a woman could be better than a man on the tennis court. Bobby would have had to eat his words, and he most definitely wouldn't have subjected himself to the humiliation and embarrassment of losing to a woman again.

However, a win from Margaret wouldn't have advanced the women's liberation movement. As I've already pointed out, Margaret didn't believe in the cause; she simply wasn't the female athlete most capable of carrying the banner of equality for women. If she'd won, Billie Jean King wouldn't have had the platform she needed to shed light on her cause. But Margaret lost, and that didn't sit well with Billie Jean. If Billie Jean wanted to advance the liberation of women, on the court or off, she would have to do it on her own. Because of the outcome of the Mother's Day Massacre, she still had something to prove. She had no choice—she had to play Bobby Riggs.

During one of her presentations, Billie Jean suggested that if she had "lost [her] match to Bobby, it would have set the women's liberation movement back fifty years." At the time, I didn't really know what the match meant for women's liberation. In fact, I barely understood what the term *women's liberation* meant. But, looking back from today, I argue that if

Margaret had defeated Bobby, it would have set the women's liberation movement back twenty-five years. Margaret would have simply curtsied and taken her prize money, denying that her win had anything to do with a bigger cause. Without a spokesperson, the movement would have been slowed, or maybe even silenced.

Ironic, isn't it? A woman who didn't believe in women's liberation unintentionally and significantly contributed to its advancement.

Chapter 6

Setting the Record Straight

*A*s I worked on the scrapbooks, I did not spend much time reflecting on the importance of the Billie Jean King match in relation to that of the Margaret Court match. I was far too busy clipping, pasting and sniffing glue. But, over the years, I have thought about this question much more, and, even though I understand the significance of the Battle of the Sexes, I believe the Mother's Day Massacre was more important.

Nevertheless, the Battle of the Sexes was a watershed television event. Because I was there in person, I didn't see the battle on live television, but I have since watched the taped version. The broadcast opened with the song "Anything You Can Do, I Can Do Better." The camera work was horrible, since it came from only one vantage point (that's right, only one camera was used), and many of the rallies were missed because the camera was focused on filming the celebrities in the crowd. In addition, at the match's conclusion, ABC failed to cover any of the post-match press conference, opting instead to go immediately to regularly scheduled programming. The poor camera work and lack of post-match coverage didn't please viewers. Apparently, ABC received thousands of complaints about its failure to cover the press conference, mainly from women. Many of them suggested it was a chauvinistic plot devised by the male-dominated ABC leadership, which the women claimed didn't want to show Bobby eating crow after his loss.

And yet, perhaps ABC's decision was a good thing. My dear friend Jerry Gross, then a CBS correspondent here in San Diego, asked Billie Jean the first question, something to the effect of "Now that you have beaten Bobby, would you be willing to make this a best two-out-of-three series?" While I don't have Billie Jean's exact reply, it was something to the tune of "What kind of question is that? Who let this guy in the room?"

Today, I find myself more interested in the statistics of the live audience and television viewers than in the actual details of the event. To put the match's viewership in perspective, consider this: The day before the Battle of the Sexes, my favorite baseball team, the San Diego Padres, had played a doubleheader against the Houston Astros in the Astrodome. The doubleheader wasn't part of the regular schedule—the game had been moved back one day for the sole purpose of accommodating the Battle of the Sexes. I was in attendance to watch the teams split the doubleheader, along with what was reported to be 5,487 other attendees. Compare that to the 30,472 at the tennis match. Now at any given time, I would estimate that almost half of the 5,488 in attendance at the doubleheader were disguised as empty seats; that is to say, there couldn't have been more than 3,000 people at the baseball games at any given time.

Moving on, let's look at the makeup of the two crowds. Typical of a sporting event in 1973, attendees of the doubleheader were predominantly male; perhaps 10 percent were female. On the contrary, at the Battle of Sexes the next night, in the same stadium, I can safely estimate from my observation that the female component was at least 40 percent. I had been to many sporting events in my young life, and this male/female composition was startling at the time. It was something I, and I suspect no one else in attendance, had ever seen before.

It's claimed that the Battle of the Sexes was watched by fifty million in the United States, with an estimated ninety million viewers worldwide. This level of US viewership was reported to be nearly double the average number of Monday Night Football viewers, which, at the time, was the highest-rated sports program in the country. In fact, the Trendex overnight returns showed the Battle of the Sexes to be rated slightly above the 33.6 number the Oakland-Cincinnati football telecast had achieved the previous October. It had been the highest-ranked Monday Night Football game in history.

The Battle of the Sexes also outdrew, by almost a six-to-one margin, the television viewership of a very important major league baseball pennant-race game between the Pittsburgh Pirates and the New York Mets, played earlier in the same week. This is about the same ratio as the tennis match's attendance compared to that of the doubleheader.

I bring these statistics up because the numbers are staggering. Why did the Battle of the Sexes get such huge numbers?

In my humble opinion, as Bobby Riggs's scrapbook maker and as a reader of virtually every piece of material written and published about the man in 1973, the Battle of the Sexes was the first sporting event in the history of this country that was watched not just by the males of the household but by daughters, mothers, grandmothers and girlfriends. It was the women who pushed the viewership over the top. It wasn't because women favored tennis over baseball or football. It was because this was an opportunity for them to come out of the kitchen and prove that they were equal to, if not better than, men. Women of all ages relished the chance to say, "I told you so," and they rooted for the one woman who had the power to show the world they had much more to offer than raising babies and making home-cooked meals. To them, this wasn't merely a tennis match—it had the potential to be a pivotal event that would affect their future, and the future of their daughters and granddaughters. They might finally get the recognition they deserved. Some were already involved in the women's movement; those who weren't couldn't help but find the enthusiasm contagious.

By challenging Billie Jean King, Bobby Riggs seemingly intended to set women back twenty-five years. Ironically, the challenge instead catapulted the women's movement to new heights. There is no doubt that women's liberation advanced by light-years in the mere two and a half hours it took to complete the match. Not only had Billie Jean beat Bobby handily, but she also won $100,000—at the time the largest purse in tennis history. Holding out from Bobby's first offer of $5,000 had paid huge dividends. Billie Jean's Virginia Slims series also received a huge boost in popularity and, ultimately, a significant increase in prize money.

For the first time in the history of sports, women had won the bragging rights. In addition, a "tennis boom" followed the Battle of the Sexes. Tennis became the sport with the largest female participation in the country, surpassing golf. Billie Jean King was the idol of women everywhere. The blue suede Adidas tennis shoes she wore during the historic match became the best-selling tennis shoe in history.

In one day, Billie Jean had changed the lives of females everywhere. And in one day, she also altered her own life forever, in ways she never could have foreseen at the time.

And what about Bobby Riggs? For his remaining twenty-two years on the planet—and beyond—he would be remembered as the guy who lost a tennis match to a girl. By instigating and then losing the contest, he did more for women's liberation than quite possibly any man before or after.

And, how did it affect me? Well, by winning, Billie Jean King had put me out of business—or had she?

Over the years, I have seen myths built up around the Battle of the Sexes. After my scrapbooking experience and years of reflection on the subject, I feel it is important to dispel these myths, not only to set the record straight but also to explain the lessons I learned from Bobby Riggs.

The first myth is that Bobby knew he was going to lose the match. If he had expected to lose, would he have challenged

Billie Jean in the first place? I don't think so. It's also been reported that Billie Jean thought she would lose—but again, if so, why did she agree to participate?

Others contend, to this day, that the match was fixed. But, I knew Bobby rather well, and I can confidently say that he would have not agreed to play a fixed match—unless he was slated to be the victor. Sure, Bobby loved being the center of attention, especially in an event of this caliber, but he wasn't stupid. He never wagered a bet unless the odds were on his side. When confronted by the press about why he didn't play the slot machines in Vegas, Bobby said that he only gambled on a sure thing. The odds of winning at the slot machines were simply too low for him. Knowing that Bobby bet on himself to win the Battle of the Sexes, and knowing how much he loved to win and hated to lose, there is no doubt in my mind this match was not fixed. Hopefully, we can lay that theory to rest.

I have read many times over that straight tennis rules were not applied in the Battle of the Sexes. This claim was an attempt by Bobby's fans to justify his loss—after all, he had annihilated Margaret Court, whose career record dominated Billie Jean's. But all one has to do is watch the tape to know that this claim is totally false. No, Bobby did not get only one serve. No, Billie Jean could not hit into the doubles alleys.

The rules were not changed to favor "the weaker sex." In fact, this match utilized the men's rule of the best-three-sets-out-of-five, which should have been a disadvantage to Billie Jean. In women's tournaments, competitors always played the best two-out-of-three sets. In my opinion, this makes Billie Jean's victory even more remarkable.

For the record, I will agree that Bobby did have one disadvantage in the match: The carpeted court that was laid over the floor of the Astrodome. This softer surface kept the balls from bouncing very high and prevented them from accelerating when they did bounce. This allowed the younger and fitter Billie Jean to wear Bobby down and, ultimately, out. And Bobby was wearing his hot and cumbersome Sugar Daddy jacket, which also hurt his ability to play.

The next myth I'd like to dispel is the most ridiculous proposition of all—that Bobby Riggs lost to Billie Jean King on purpose, because he bet against himself. This is preposterous. It's outside any realm of the imagination that Bobby intentionally threw that match or any other. Winning was embedded in Bobby's psyche. He thrived on the thrill of the chase and the rush of adrenaline that came with it. He couldn't conceive of losing. One only needs look at Bobby's history to see that this claim doesn't hold up to scrutiny. The only money Bobby made on the Mother's Day Massacre was the money he bet on himself, as his self-serving agent at the time, Jackie Barnett, took advantage of Bobby. And, let's not forget that Bobby made his first fortune betting on himself in London at Wimbledon in 1939. After winning the Wimbledon gamble, Bobby was bit by the betting bug, and, usually, he was on the winning end. And trust me, Bobby was betting heavily on himself to win, in the hours leading up to the Battle of the Sexes. If he made any money on that match, it was solely through the sponsorships and promotions leading up to it.

In fact, Bobby was apparently so certain he would beat Billie Jean that his loss left him despondent. According to my Uncle John, Bobby locked himself in the bathroom in his hotel room for such a long time after the match that his entourage was concerned about him—he actually didn't come out for four hours. His behavior makes perfect sense. After all, Bobby was an accomplished tennis player and self-promoter. He would have never achieved the success he did in life or in tennis if he had mastered the concept of losing gracefully. Intentionally losing went against everything Bobby stood for—it wasn't even an option. Instead, Bobby shamelessly bet on himself to win. "All my life everything has been a contest," he said. "This so turns me on, and I so love it—I love the competition—and that's the thing I crave, like some guys crave women. I crave the game."

While I stress Bobby's obsession with winning, he also knew that losing was part of the game. Even in the face of humiliation, Bobby was humble enough to publicly praise Billie Jean. In an interview with *The New York Times*, he was quoted as saying, "She was too good. She played too well. She was playing well within herself, and I couldn't get the most out of my game."

In addition, while Bobby was handsomely compensated for the Battle of the Sexes (most of which he probably lost in bets he placed on himself), his defeat lost him a much-desired opportunity to score an even larger financial windfall. You see, beating Billie Jean King was just the next step in Bobby's big payday plan. If he had been victorious, he would have been able to continue his winning trend by challenging other female tennis pros. Next in his sights was America's tennis darling, Chris Evert. In 1973, Chrissie, as she was known, was still a rising star and one of the youngest females on the professional circuit. America had quickly fallen in love with her the previous year, when, at the age of seventeen, she won the 1972 Virginia Slims series. A prospective Chris Evert encounter would have been worth millions of dollars to Bobby. He would have never taken a fall with such a significant financial motivation on the horizon.

There is another myth deserving of correction. Rumor had it that Bobby and Chris Evert had also made a deal to play each other, either before or after he played Billie Jean. I even included articles announcing this agreement in Bobby's scrapbooks. However, I'm here to lay this rumor to rest. Chris Evert, herself, confirmed its falseness by a response to an email inquiry from me in August of 2012—proof that you cannot believe everything you read.

Among these myths are facts—one of which is that money was of great interest to Bobby. He had just divorced Priscilla and received a great deal of money in the settlement, making him a "retired millionaire," as he put it. However, his love for money was equally matched, and sometimes surpassed, by his quest to be at the center of attention. Sure, Bobby loved tennis, but one reason he loved it so much was that it brought him fame. I'm convinced that his desire to return to the center stage was the primary reason he spent two years relentlessly pestering Billie Jean to take him up on his challenge.

An article from a couple of years after Bobby's defeat best illustrates this point. In September of 1973, Bobby was given feature placement in *Sports Illustrated*. After being defeated in the Battle of the Sexes, however, he suffered a two-year lapse in coverage from the magazine. His next appearance in its pages came in 1975, and the reason for it was most likely a publicity stunt Bobby spearheaded solely for the purpose of returning to the spotlight.

Titled "The Death Valley Hustle," this article covered Bobby in yet another duel—and yes, another bet—this time revolving around a running match. Bobby had challenged Bill Emmerton, the great Australian ultra-distance running champion, to a race through Death Valley. Not surprisingly, the odds were clearly in Bobby's favor. According to the contest rules, Bobby would have to run twenty-five miles at a faster time than the champion could run fifty. With his Bosom Buddies in tow, Bobby won by a whopping forty minutes. Given these rather ridiculous odds, and the fact that there wasn't a pot of gold awaiting the winner at the finish line, publicity had to have been Bobby's primary motive. And, surprisingly, it worked; *Sports Illustrated* actually thought the race newsworthy. Bobby made great copy, even if his promotional events were far from dramatic. As far as Bobby was concerned, his goal was accomplished. Considering the respective results, Bobby's concluding quote in the article was odd: "Playing Billie Jean was a cakewalk compared to this."

However, Bobby's brother wasn't buying it. A well-read man, Uncle John kept abreast of the news, whether it was politics or sports. He was also a regular subscriber to *Sports Illustrated*. Whenever I visited my aunt and uncle at their Coronado home, Uncle John would hand me the copies of the magazine he had finished reading so I could read them, too. Sometimes, we'd comment on the articles and the athletes featured in them. This pattern took a turn, though, when the issue covering Bobby's race against Bill Emmerton came out. Instead of handing me the magazine as usual, Uncle John slammed it on the floor with disgust and bellowed in his deep, booming voice, "You won't believe what Bobby did to get in this piece of crap! I told him he's turning into a goddamn circus clown."

Resorting to jogging across Death Valley with well-endowed Bosom Buddies for the sake of such menial publicity fell far below the ever-increasing standard Uncle John had set for his brother. I, on the other hand, viewed the article from an entirely different perspective. Being seventeen, I greatly enjoyed the accompanying photos—the desert can be so lovely.

Many people have painted Bobby as the villain of the women's liberation movement. While it is true Bobby actually said, "Women should be kept barefoot and pregnant," and,

"A woman's place is in the kitchen and the bedroom—and not necessarily in that order," I question whether the ensuing criticism is warranted. Frankly, I don't think Bobby believed any of the derogatory statements he made about women. He was just playing the part of ultimate self-promoter; his main goals in life were to be the center of attention and to make money.

As self-promoter extraordinaire, Bobby's job was to create as much interest, publicity and fascination around himself as he possibly could. Bobby was a smart man, and over the course of the years, he found that there was something to be said for shock value. He learned to say whatever would attract a gaggle of reporters or would bring cameras and talking heads in his direction—the more controversial, the better.

Behind the outrageous persona, I believe Bobby actually respected many women, even though he hid it very well. He treated my Auntie Bun and my mother, Dolores, with respect and courtesy, to the point that my mom was never quite certain whether Bobby's public persona was an act. And, his first two tennis coaches, Eleanor Tennant and Esther Bartosh, were women. Because they were instrumental in making him the great player he was, he was well aware that women knew tennis and could play the game well.

What a racket!

13-1 – BUT RIGGS WINS

Bobby personified: entering a court with an oversized racket on the left, and playing an entire team on the other side of the net.

I believe that Bobby also had to have had some level of respect for the intellectual abilities of the opposite sex. I cannot count how many times Uncle John told me that yet another woman had taken Bobby for money. For example, according to my Uncle John, Ruth Wells wound up with the house in La Jolla after her break-up with Bobby. Being the hustler he was, Bobby had to inwardly admire a woman who was able to outsmart him.

Then, there was Billie Jean King. While some might contend that they were steadfast enemies, their rivalry turned into mutual respect and a close friendship that lasted for the twenty-two years Bobby lived after losing to her. In his prime, Bobby would have never publicly divulged his admiration or respect for women. Yes, he played the villain's role to perfection, but I believe he was simply milking it for all the money and publicity he could get. That's what Bobby did, and he did it well.

As a scrapbook-making fourteen- and then fifteen-year-old, I know it was impossible for me—and I am convinced for anyone else at the time—to see the historical significance of these events. Amidst the carnival atmosphere surrounding the Battle of the Sexes and the major influx of world and national events that bombarded the news during the same year, I simply don't see how anybody could have seen the historical significance of those events. There was far too much going on in the world for anybody to calculate historical context so quickly: Roe v. Wade, the start of Watergate, the end of the Vietnam War, the women's liberation movement—which followed closely on the heels of the civil rights movement— were all happening, and a swell of other headlines pelted the

American public on a daily basis. Furthermore, the historical context of the match depended too much on Billie Jean's post-Battle of the Sexes path. Any attempt to predict the importance of her win shortly after it happened would have been based on guesswork, not on foresight or analysis.

For example, what if Billie Jean King had not been named one of *Life* magazine's "100 Most Important Americans of the 20th Century"? What difference would it have made if she hadn't received the 1999 Arthur Ashe Courage Award or led the exemplary work of the Women's Sports Foundation? Would the match's impact on history have been lessened if the United States Tennis Association's National Tennis Center had been dedicated in someone else's name? What if Billie Jean hadn't been honored with the Champion of Justice Award from the Public Justice Foundation or received the prestigious Presidential Medal of Freedom in 2009?

While any one of these events might not have altered history on its own, together they certainly carried some weight. If Billie Jean had quietly faded away from the scene due to tennis injuries (of which she had many) or due to her assistant, Marilyn Barnett, disclosing their same-sex affair, would history look the same forty years later? I can't conceive of a scenario in which that's possible. While it was Bobby Riggs' prematch promotional stunts that created the phenomenal interest in the Battle of the Sexes, it was Billie Jean King's post-match accolades and presence that made the event legendary.

Last, but certainly not least, is the misconception that the Battle of the Sexes and Title IX, the "equal participation" legislation that celebrated its fortieth anniversary in June 2012, were somehow connected. Some say that the Mother's Day Massacre and/or the Battle of the Sexes played a role in the passing of the legislation, but given the chronology of the events, this cannot be true. Title IX was signed by President Richard Nixon on June 23, 1972—about a year before either tennis match was played. Some also contend that Title IX contributed to Billie Jean King's fight for equal pay for female tennis pros. If it did, it was indirectly. Billie Jean's push for equality on the tennis court wasn't due to a law or a federal program—it was based on a belief originating from the women's liberation movement.

Title IX had nothing to do with Bobby Riggs, Billie Jean King or tennis. The legislation was designed to ensure equal participation by both sexes in federally funded programs. Led by Congresswomen Patsy Mink (D-Hawaii) and Edith Green (D-Oregon) and Senator Birch Bayh (D-Indiana), the bill finally passed the floor in early 1972, after many years of impassioned debate and several defeats. But, any application

Title IX had to college athletics came later—separately, distinct from and after the Mother's Day Massacre and the Battle of the Sexes.

Title IX has influenced my life, but back in the early 1970s, it had little, if any, impact on either tennis or me. However, in retrospect, it's apparent that the near-concurrent timing of the bill's passing and the tennis matches definitely created momentum and focus for the cause of equal opportunity and participation. There is no doubt Title IX opened doors and created opportunities that were once not afforded to women. The 2012 Olympics are a perfect example. We looked on in pride as the United States led in medal winners, and it did not escape my attention that the majority of our country's victors were female. These female champions are the daughters of Title IX and followers in the footsteps of women like Ann Meyers (now Drysdale), the great US Olympic basketball player who, in 1972, became the first female to win an athletic scholarship from a United States university (UCLA).

In my lifetime, women's participation in sports has evolved significantly. The large and small triumphs of these women have paved the way for future generations. Often, we take these victories for granted or we forget or aren't even aware of the historic breakthroughs that advanced females in the world of athletics. Billie Jean King's win was one triumph for womankind that won't soon be forgotten. However, there are others that make us realize it wasn't all that long ago that women pushed beyond the "gentlemen only, ladies forbidden" barriers designed to stifle their abilities and limit them to the life of housewife and mother.

Marathon running is a perfect example. I took up long-distance endurance running later in life (though absent of any Bosom Buddies), and, while running the Boston Marathon, I found out about one such breakthrough. It was April 16, 2012, and the second time I'd competed in this particular race. While the record-breaking heat made it unforgettable, I'll also never forget my shock at discovering that this day marked only the fortieth anniversary of women being allowed to run the Boston Marathon, which is now almost 120 years old.

The first woman to reach that milestone was Kathrine Switzer. Although, it was 1972 before the rules changed, Switzer actually first ran in the Boston Marathon in 1967. She used good old ingenuity to buck the system, listing her name as "K.V. Switzer" on the registration. And, she bypassed the physical exam by claiming she'd already been cleared. (You've got to admire a woman with that kind of spunk.) Once it came out that she was indeed a woman, organizer Jock Semple caught up to her mid-race and attempted to push her off the track, screaming for her to "get out of my race and give me those numbers." With the help of her boyfriend, Kathrine pushed Semple off the track instead, and she finished in four hours and twenty minutes. She waited to enter the race again until she could do so on an official basis in 1972.

Putting this historic event in the context of my own life helped me realize its significance. My half-sister, Janet (from my father's first marriage), was a college student at San Jose State University in 1972. I find it inconceivable that, had she been inclined to try, Janet would not have been allowed to enter any pre-1972 Boston Marathon simply because she is a woman.

Over the last four decades, the memory of the first woman to run in the Boston Marathon has dimmed, but the number of females who participate in the sport of running has grown exponentially. In the United States, running has now surpassed tennis as the sport with the largest female participation. By 2011, almost 60 percent of entrants in US running events were female. In what was once a male-only sport, it is women who now dominate. Once that door opened, women ran right through it, eager for the opportunity to enjoy an activity that not too long before had been forbidden to them.

Although it shouldn't have, it took a series of prominent events to change the male-only mindset that dominated the world of sports. Title IX was certainly one of them. So were events like the Mother's Day Massacre and the Battle of the Sexes and other successes by such strong women as Billie Jean King and Kathrine Switzer. Eventually, these events and people opened opportunities for females everywhere as schools and organizations recognized females as viable athletes and credible contenders. My high school joined in the recognition of female athletes by adding girls' sports to its program. By the time I graduated in June 1976, the girls' program had grown to approximately the same size as the boys' program.

Women's liberation even affected my household. Bored by more than twenty years of homemaking, my mother, Dolores, went back to work as a psychiatric nurse when I was a senior in high school.

Women had, indeed, come a long way. And, just to set the record straight, I truly believe that, by challenging female tennis players, Bobby Riggs did, indeed, help them get there.

Chapter 7

Play Smart

*M*y gig as scrapbook maker taught me about much more than Bobby Riggs' career—it taught me about life, politics, sports and work. It was an education that went far beyond the classroom, and in some ways, far beyond my years. Undeniably, the lessons I learned that year have followed me throughout my life.

The first thing I learned was to take everything I have and give it all to whatever it is I am doing. In other words, I learned to have zero tolerance for taking shortcuts or doing just enough to get by. I credit my Uncle John for embedding in me this work ethic. A staunch perfectionist, he demanded the same from others, including me. I knew this when I accepted the job. There was an expectation that the finished scrapbooks would be professional and meet Uncle John's standard of excellence. They would be like trophies, and everybody associated would be proud to show them to other people. I got that message loud and clear. Anything less than perfection would be unacceptable. The quality and detail of the scrapbooks and indices were borne out of this expectation.

Certainly, I have applied this lesson to my subsequent career as a CPA, where excellence is a constant requirement, especially given the subject matter I specialize in—estate, gift and trust issues. I assist very wealthy families in reducing risk and staying wealthy. As I will discuss in a later chapter, my professional training proved invaluable when I was called on to assist in the making of a documentary about the Battle of the Sexes.

However, my time with Bobby wasn't totally free of regrets. Immediately, I can think of two things I would've done differently. First, I wound up with multiple copies of almost every article I glued into the scrapbooks, given that I received the same articles from multiple sources (especially those distributed by the Associated Press). If I could do it over again, I would have made scrapbooks for myself from the extras, because while I do possess a significant amount of memorabilia, the original books are no longer in my possession.

My second regret is that the scrapbooks contain material related only to Bobby Riggs, the Mother's Day Massacre, and the Battle of the Sexes.

Giving it my all as a scrapbook maker forced me to read about a lot more than just Bobby. I was compelled to scan all the articles in the hundreds of newspapers and magazines from which I was clipping content. Thus, as I became an expert on the man, I also became an expert in the events of 1973, a year that I believe was as important to American social and political history, as the Battle of the Sexes was to sports history. However, the scrapbooks are completely devoid of any articles related to US or world affairs or politics. Any references to larger news stories contained therein are strictly parenthetical. If I could do it all over again, I would have made scrapbooks that covered all of the remarkable events of 1973. Since it took two minutes for the glue to dry, I got to read about Watergate, women's liberation, Roe vs. Wade, and the end of the Vietnam War—and I got to do this reading outside of the school setting. I suspect my straight A's were due, in part, to this extracurricular education.

1973 was a busy and tumultuous year, and not just on the tennis court. During that year, historic figures fell in disgrace, stars were born, and legends were made. A multitude of records were set, wars were ended, and rules were changed.

It was a good year for civil rights and liberties—in it, Ernie Banks technically became the first black manager in baseball, the Supreme Court granted equal rights to females serving in the military, and a lawsuit was filed in Detroit challenging the Little League's no-girls-allowed rule. In the 131 days between and including the Mother's Day Massacre on May 13 and the Battle of the Sexes on September 20, there was enough news to make these tennis matches—historically important and ingeniously marketed as they were—seem inconsequential.

The year began with President Richard Nixon's second inauguration. From there, the political news just kept coming and coming. Nixon henchmen H. R. Haldeman and John Ehrlichman resigned, soon to be followed by Attorney General Richard Kleindienst. Then, White House counsel John Dean was fired. These turnovers, and the events surrounding them, captured the attention of the *Washington Post*'s Bob Woodward and Carl Bernstein, and as a result of their investigation, the newspaper won a Pulitzer Prize for extraordinary reporting.

To the great relief of many, the increasingly unpopular Vietnam War finally ended. A cease-fire agreement between the United States and North Vietnam was announced, and within days, the military draft ended. Many families—mine included—viewed this news with great joy and relief. While we were a military family (my father had served in both World War II and in Korea, rising to the rank of lieutenant commander in the US Navy, and he also served in the Naval

Reserves during the Vietnam War), the end of the war and of the draft preceded my brother's sixteenth birthday by less than two months, giving him the opportunity to enjoy his last two years of high school without the prospect of mandatory service hanging over his head. Our cousin, Ronnie, had lost his leg in Vietnam combat and then committed suicide due to depression when he returned to the States. Shortly following the cease-fire, the first US prisoners of war were released to US authorities near Hanoi and soon returned home to American soil at California's Travis Air Force Base. The last of our soldiers left Vietnam on March 29, or so we were led to believe.

Around the same time, all state laws preventing a woman's right to an abortion during the first three months of her pregnancy were ruled unconstitutional by the Supreme Court in the landmark Roe v. Wade case. Almost forty years later, the national debate on this topic carries on with great fervor.

In sports, CBS (the network that broadcast the Mother's Day Massacre) sold the New York Yankees to George Steinbrenner for $10 million (now, there's a great investment!), and the Miami Dolphins defeated the Washington Redskins in Super Bowl VII to cap off the one and only undefeated NFL season. In boxing, George Foreman, Billie Jean King's impromptu bodyguard at the Battle of the Sexes, defeated Joe Frazier to win his first heavyweight-boxing championship.

The Watergate hearings, lead by Senator Sam Ervin, began on May 17, 1973. In short order, the White House admitted that virtually every presidential meeting had been taped. W. Mark Felt, later identified as "Deep Throat," resigned from the FBI. Then Henry Kissinger was named secretary of state. A staunch Nixon supporter, my Uncle John was mortified by the avalanche of bad news emanating from the White House.

On the international front, Chilean dictator Salvador Allende was killed in a coup, and the United Nations accepted both East Germany and West Germany as member nations. In addition, the American people got to witness history happen, as Leonid Brezhnev became the first Soviet leader to appear on US television.

And the nation mourned on the evening of September 20, when recording artist Jim Croce passed away in a plane crash. That event forever linked him, at least in my mind, with the Battle of the Sexes. His song "Leroy Brown" was one of my favorites.

I remember reading a lot about other sports before and during the Battle of the Sexes. Secretariat became the first horse in twenty-five years to win the Triple Crown, and the New York Knicks upset the Wilt Chamberlain-led Los Angeles Lakers to win the NBA crown. Nolan Ryan was ringing up huge strikeout totals in baseball, and Hank Aaron set the record for the most home runs in a single league. Willie Mays announced his retirement on September 20, the same day the Battle of the Sexes took place. In the boxing world, Muhammad Ali and George Foreman were heavyweight champions.

There was no shortage of news to fill the papers in 1973, a fact that made some journalists famous and gave others job security. Yet, with all the newsworthy accomplishments, records and upsets, the coverage wasn't equal—at least, not in Houston newspapers. Feeding off the hype and hoopla Bobby was building, Houston's press focused primarily on tennis and the events leading up to the Battle of the Sexes.

There were 102 days left in the year, when Billie Jean put Bobby out of business. Given the huge backlog of clippings that built up during the Battle of the Sexes, I stayed busy on the scrapbooks until early 1974. During that time, Spiro Agnew resigned as vice president of the United States, and Gerald R. Ford became the first unelected person to fill that role in the history of our nation. Soon, calls for President Nixon's impeachment become loud and clear, and Nixon responded by adamantly telling the Associated Press, "I am not a crook."

Internationally, war broke out between Israel and both Egypt and Syria, a conflict that became known as "the Second Arab-Israeli War." However, by Halloween, outmanned Egyptian and Syrian forces had accepted a United Nations cease-fire agreement.

On the home front, my brother, Bob, had turned sixteen and learned how to drive. To celebrate his feat, in late 1973, my family nominated him to be the one who got to wait in long lines at gas stations to fill up the family cars. By October, OPEC had begun its oil embargo against the West.

And, let's not forget celestial news, as 1973's headlines were not limited to planet Earth: Pioneer 10 sent back the first-ever close-up color photographs of Jupiter, just a few weeks after the Mariner 10 became the first vehicle ever to launch for Mercury (successfully passing close by the planet in 1974).

I kept up with the world of sports after the Battle of the Sexes. By documenting the event, I felt I had gained insights into the world of athletics that none of my friends shared. After the Battle of the Sexes, Bobby and his outrageous quotes quickly faded from the sports pages. However, the headlines were soon replaced with accolades of other great athletes. The New York Mets finished an incredible stretch-run pennant drive to capture first place in the National League East, and then upset Pete Rose's heavily favored Big Red Machine from Cincinnati in the National League playoffs, only to be defeated by the Oakland A's in a thrilling and very well-pitched seven-game World Series. O.J. Simpson became the first NFL player to ever rush for 2,000 yards, and Jack Nicklaus became the world's first golfer to earn $2 million in a single year. And last, but definitely not least, New Jersey became the first state in the nation to allow girls to play Little League baseball.

Yes, the world was busy. It was a year of heroes, both rising and falling, and the events that surrounded them changed the lives of many and influenced world leaders and public perception.

It was also the year that the American Psychiatric Association removed homosexuality from its list of psychological disorders. At the time this was not perceived to be of any relevance to her, but Billie Jean King most likely applauded the move. Down the road, her sexuality would present its own obstacles. A few years after her victory over Bobby, Billie Jean drew the public's fascination when her former assistant, Marilyn Barnett, unveiled Billie Jean's sexual orientation by filing a palimony lawsuit against her. At the time, Billie Jean was married to a man, Lawrence "Larry" King (no, not the TV personality).

The year also brought us (in no particular order): the first worldwide telecast by an entertainer (Elvis Presley in Hawaii), which was watched by more people than the Apollo moon landing (I watched both events); the deaths of President Lyndon B. Johnson and the infamous Pablo Picasso; the unveiling of the new London Bridge; the building of the world's tallest skyscraper (the Sears Tower in Chicago); the kidnapping of J. Paul Getty's grandson; the establishment of the Drug Enforcement Agency; the unprecedented marriage of Princess Anne to a commoner (Captain Mark Phillips); and the passing of the Endangered Species Act. And, lest I forget, 1973 was the year Bruce Springsteen released his first best-selling album, *The Wild, the Innocent, and the E Street Shuffle*, which, to this day, I listen to regularly.

And I read about most, if not all, of these historic events in periodicals I clipped from. While that may not seem like a remarkable achievement for those who peruse newspapers from cover to cover, it was uncommon for a high school freshman and then sophomore. Plus, you have to keep in mind that I was not only reading the local newspaper; I was reading papers that came from one coast to the other, and some from overseas. Each contained its own accounts of these events, and over time, I became well versed in the details that impacted so many lives, including mine. I'll go so far as to claim that I suspect there haven't been many years in US history that were more significant than 1973. However, I do acknowledge the bias inherent in my opinion; my life didn't revolve around the news in earlier or later years like it did in 1973. While I was gluing articles into Bobby's scrapbooks, that year was being glued into my DNA. The stories and the details surrounding them remain there to this day.

I don't regret being a student of the world's news, nor do I regret making the scrapbooks. Both experiences have educated me, molded my opinions and opened my eyes to the world around me—with all its greatness and faults.

My desire to have a copy of the scrapbooks, as well as scrapbooks chronicling the rest of that year's news, isn't solely selfish. It stems from my belief that the historical significance of the two tennis matches can be truly understood only in context of the maelstrom that was the world in 1973. It's obvious that women's liberation and Roe v. Wade are two of the year's topics that relate in some way to these two matches, but when you look at the news from a non-tennis angle, it's also apparent that 1973 was a year of upheaval and change. The abundance of news signifying major beginnings and endings represented a new world order. Therefore, the Mother's Day Massacre and the Battle of the Sexes seemed to fit perfectly with the tumultuous and transformational occurrences brought to us that year. But, is that something that any of us who watched these two tennis matches would have known at the time? I cannot see how this would be possible. Again, the ability to look back in time through a different lens enables us to see these events on a much broader scope.

Yet, I feel like I was a part of this year in history. My role as scrapbook maker thrust me into a world that I'd only been remotely aware of in my young and rather sheltered life. I would guess that few people my age knew as much as I did about wars, world events or sports. I certainly got quite an education in the lives and careers of politicians and celebrities, and in the causes and movements that changed our country and the world.

Since my scrapbooking days, I've had the privilege of meeting some of the people who shaped the news that year. For example, just recently, I ran into Jim Croce's widow, Ingrid, at the huge art show known as Art San Diego. And, in July of 2012, at an event at La Valencia Hotel in La Jolla, I was the catalyst—along with my radio show partner, Joe Vecchio—for the unveiling of a plaque commemorating the prolific children's book author Dr. Seuss. The plaque was installed above a booth where he always sat, in a restaurant that had been his favorite for forty-five years. There, I chatted with Alexander Butterfield, the former Nixon White House aide who, in July of 1973, informed the United States Senate Watergate Committee that President Richard Nixon had, indeed, secretly recorded multitudes of conservations. Best of all, in February 2013, I interviewed the great comedian Don Rickles on my radio show, almost forty years after he had interviewed Bobby Riggs on *The Tonight Show*; Mr. Rickles had been filling in for the vacationing Johnny Carson. At the age of fourteen or fifteen, I would never have dreamed that I would come face to face with these famous people.

The standing joke at my house, where my youngest child, Demi, is now a high-school junior, is that all significant events in United States and world history have some connection to the year 1973. In some ways, this may very well be true—however, I admit that my extensive knowledge of the events of that year, and my willingness to share it, may have influenced my perceptions just a bit. But, like I said, there is a ring of truth to the joke.

For example, Demi's history teacher asked her class to name the only professional athlete to ever be drafted by major league baseball, football and basketball teams. As many of you might know, the correct answer is Dave Winfield. In what year did that occur? The answer is 1973, of course.

From left to right: Richard with his daughter, Demi, Billie Jean and his radio show partner, Joe.

Then, when Demi's musical theater class watched *La Cage aux Folles*, it was pointed out that this musical was the first production in which a same-sex couple publicly sang a love duet. I asked Demi, "In what year did author Jean Poiret write this play?" Indeed, it was none other than 1973.

If, in conversation with me, you should bring up a topic relating in any way to the year 1973, you will not get another word in for at least one hour. And, if you mention the Mother's Day Massacre and/or the Battle of the Sexes, better make that two hours. If your topic has nothing to do with 1973, I will try to find a way to make the connection—and I'm just as likely to succeed as not. I'm well aware of my compulsion to recite the events of that year. I even find I am receiving fewer and fewer social invitations as the fortieth anniversaries of these tennis matches draw near. My affinity for relating anything and everything to 1973 doesn't appear to be waning—so consider yourself warned. However, if you should ever draw "1973" when playing Trivial Pursuit, give me a call!

I wasn't the only one in the family who possessed an interest in the news. My Uncle John was very interested in politics and world affairs. When I was in the process of scouring newspapers for any tidbit related to his brother, he noticed I was becoming quite the expert on world events. Before long, our conversations began to take on a similar pattern. Uncle John would ask me about some event in the news, usually concerning national politics or world affairs. Then, he'd follow his inquiry with the same request: "Dick, give me a full report." I'd gladly tell him everything I knew. I never disappointed my uncle in 1973; however, the years before and after were an entirely different story.

Although Bobby was Uncle John's brother, the two had very different interests. Bobby didn't have much, if any, interest in hearing or talking about the news—in fact, I doubt he paid much attention to anybody on the planet that year not named Margaret or Billie Jean. This attribute wasn't one Bobby reserved solely for 1973—his laser-focus on the tasks he wanted to accomplish was his standard MO. As far as I know, his indifference to world affairs remained with him for the rest of his life.

It's not that Bobby didn't care about anything—he did. And, when he cared about something, he gave it his all, just as I learned to do. He cared about tennis, and his achievements confirm that. But, he also had other interests: namely, advancing his favorite brand, the Bobby Riggs brand. At times, though, he was curious, and when he chose to ask a question, it was often thought provoking. Of course, in early 1974, it was Bobby who asked me the most interesting question I'd ever been asked in my life. His question retains that distinction to today.

"You Can See. Now Go Do Those Things."

"**Y**ou can see. Now go do those things."

I spoke those words to a character named Jim in a book titled *The Rise*. I was one of twenty or so co-authors on the book, and we were led by Greg S. Reid, an astounding motivational speaker and author best known for the best-selling *Three Feet from Gold*. In August of 2012, *The Rise* became an immediate (if two days is immediate in the publishing industry) bestseller on Amazon. It was an amazing team effort, one that demanded the best from each of us. As the contributor of the book's Chapter 9, I am proud of the part I played on the team. In fact, many people have mentioned that this chapter was the most important one for them.

The book's two main characters, Jim and Taz, are very uncertain about their path as they take the reader through the first eight chapters. After they meet me, though, they develop a laser-like focus as they pursue their dream of creating a documentary film that will change the world for the better. As a whole, *The Rise* is about collaboration and never giving up on one's dreams—two of the crucially important lessons I learned while putting together the Bobby Riggs scrapbooks.

Perseverance was my mantra as I completed scrapbook after scrapbook. I never allowed myself to entertain the possibility of quitting. Had I not had this persistence, Auntie Bun probably would have divorced Uncle John, who, in turn, would have disowned me. Seriously, though, because I learned that giving up was not an option, I have been blessed with the mindset of success. I keep on keeping on, even when the odds don't initially appear to be in my favor.

As I take everything I have and give it all to whatever I'm doing, I've found that the best results occur when I ask, "How may I serve?" That is what collaboration is truly all about—it is the opposite of asking, "What's in it for me?" Imagine how different the outcome would have been if I'd been more interested in what the scrapbooks could do for me than in what I could do for Bobby. I might have given up halfway through the project. Or, I might have slapped the books together haphazardly, disrespecting Bobby's legacy for selfish reasons. Thankfully, even at a young age, I realized that the way I carried out my job would have some impact on Bobby's legacy. I stayed on task, maintaining the same level of commitment to the end.

Today, my legacy includes being the father of one son and two daughters. I'm also a CPA who became an estate, gift and trust expert and a best-selling co-author, and I still look back fondly on my time as the scrapbook maker for one of the greatest tennis players in history. But, back in 1973, I wasn't playing any tennis myself. In fact, I didn't touch a tennis racket until 1980. I was a twenty-one-year-old college senior at the time, and my friend Laura sat on the bench on the women's tennis team at the University of San Diego (ah, Title IX in action). As a benchwarmer, Laura wasn't getting enough practice in, so she kept bugging me to hit tennis balls with her. I, of course, had seen a good portion of my high school life preempted by the scrapbooks, and I remained very focused and studious throughout college. In short, I wasn't getting enough action—oops, I mean I wanted to find a fun activity to participate in.

Although I had never played tennis before, my experiences with "eye-hand" sports, like table tennis, basketball and baseball, made me a very quick learner on the court. The first time I played, I used an old aluminum racket—I'll give you one guess as to who gave it to me—and immediately fell in love with the game.

Despite never having had any lessons, over the years, I became somewhat accomplished as a tennis player. In 1997, I claimed the number-one ranking in San Diego County in the 4.5 division, after being undefeated throughout the entire season and winning the championship match in the annual San Diego District tennis championships tournament. But, this ranking was not effortlessly accomplished. As much as I loved the game, I had to overcome my share of difficulties to play it.

It was late on a Saturday afternoon in September of 1995 when my middle child and oldest daughter, Mia, accidentally kicked me in the right eye. She was barely three years old and was wearing Mary Janes, a classic style of girls' shoe made of leather—in this case, a very hard leather. As luck would have it, I was also wearing something hard—a hard contact lens. The meeting of the two proved to be a very bad combination; her shoe shattered the lens under my eyelid. Over the new few hours, I gradually lost sight in that eye. I am not exaggerating when I say that the pain was excruciating.

To complicate matters—well, a couple of things complicated matters. First, it was late on a Saturday afternoon, and I quickly discovered that eye doctors were in short supply at such a time. Second, that very morning I had won a tennis match in the semifinals of the Lake Murray Tennis Club A-division championship, and I was scheduled to play in the championship finals at 9:30 the next morning.

I called my client, the late Dr. Charles May, who founded orthokeratology, a therapy designed to reshape the cornea for those with visual impairments. Finding him at home, I told him what had happened. Dr. May said he was almost certain I had suffered a retinal detachment and offered to place an immediate call to one of his friends, Dr. Larry Cooper, an eye injury specialist in downtown San Diego. Dr. Cooper called me within the hour and told me he could see me as early as I cared to be examined on Sunday morning. I told him I'd be at his place at 7:00 a.m.

Punctual and wearing my tennis clothes, I arrived at Dr. Cooper's clinic at 7:00 sharp. My tennis bag, along with my rackets and supplies, was ready and packed in the trunk of my car. After examining me, Dr. Cooper confirmed I was suffering from (and I *was* suffering) a retinal detachment. He went on to tell me he had Dr. Mark Smith, a San Diego-based retinal-detachment specialist, on call. All I had to do was go next door to Mercy Hospital, which could accept me in its surgery center immediately. Dr. Smith was just a phone call away and would meet me there.

It was great to know there was a skilled team ready to wheel me into surgery and repair the damage my daughter's shoe had done. But couldn't Dr. Cooper see that I was dressed for tennis, not surgery? He couldn't possibly think this was my normal mode of dress. When I instructed Dr. Cooper to schedule my surgery for first thing Monday morning, he didn't try to hide his disbelief that I was even contemplating playing tennis in an hour, let alone in the finals of a tournament, with only one functioning eye. After he confirmed that delaying the surgery for one day wouldn't compromise the recovery of sight in my eye, Dr. Cooper relented, against his better judgment. However, his acceptance of my terms wasn't unconditional. He made me promise to wear a cap, pulled down low on my forehead, to reduce the possibility that a ball would strike me in the eye—not the injured eye, as one might think, but rather the eye I could see with. He wanted to make sure I kept at least some of my sight.

That promise left me with a detail or two to take care of before the match—I didn't own a tennis cap and had never worn one while playing. My very next stop was the front desk of the Lake Murray Tennis Club, where I made my purchase. And I kept my word, wearing the cap during the entire match. To this day, I still play tennis with a cap pulled down low, even if it's cloudy outside.

The first challenge I faced in the championship match was my lack of depth perception. I obviously had never had to play tennis, or any other sport, with one eye. It's a skill that I now know takes more than a small amount of practice to master, but I had to quickly make adjustments to my game. I decided to play every shot my opponent hit close to the lines as if it were in. This was for two reasons—first, because I really couldn't tell whether they were truly in or out, and second, I didn't need the additional stress of worrying about whether I was "hooking" the other player with bad line calls.

The opponent was my second challenge. Tim Haar stood six foot five. With his height came a serve that boomed out of the clouds at more than a hundred miles per hour. Only two players at the club could serve harder, and I wasn't one of them. I lost the first set 6–3, and, despite still not breaking Tim's serve, stole the second set in a tiebreaker at 7–6, winning the tiebreaker at an unbelievable 12–10. My eye hurt the whole time, but I refused to forget the first lesson I learned as Bobby Riggs' scrapbook maker—that I had to put absolutely everything I had into whatever I was doing. It was going to take everything I had to win this match, which was okay by me. There would be plenty of time to rest after my eye surgery.

Tim and I traded ten games in the third set on serve, when at 30-all on Tim's serve in game 11, he double-faulted. That was the opening I needed. I took advantage of the added point to very aggressively return his next first serve to his backhand side, forcing him to hit a shot wide. After sixteen service games, I finally broke his serve to lead 6–5 in the third and deciding set. After dropping the first point of my service game, I hit consecutive aces, followed by consecutive service winners, and, similar to Billie Jean when she beat Bobby, I celebrated by throwing my racket high into the air. I was a one-eyed champion!

After the trophy presentation, the chair umpire, the late Pat Poisett—who, by the way, had known Bobby Riggs very well—approached me and said, "Richard, you were the most gracious tennis player I have ever seen in my forty years of working tennis matches. Not only did you never miss a line call, you also gave your opponent about twenty-five balls that he hit two or three inches out." Pat's compliment deserved a response and an explanation, so I revealed my peculiar circumstances to her and explained my desire to free my overwhelmed mind from the stress of calling lines. My opponent, Tim, was standing right next to me and, hearing the exchange, said, "Now I *really* feel bad"—albeit with a sense of humor. It was bad enough that the guy had lost, but now Tim knew he had lost to someone who was blind in one eye.

The injury introduced me to challenges I'd never faced on the court, but it also brought new challenges in day-to-day life. No doubt because I am a white male from a middle-class family, I had no firsthand experience in how it felt to be "different" or to have an obvious physical disability or affliction. That changed a few days after my eye surgery. My wife, Mari, suggested we take the two children we had at the time (then three and four years old) out to eat. Accessorized with a huge bandage held in place by two large strips of medical tape over my right eye, I agreed—even though the bandage was constantly stained from the ongoing drainage oozing from my eye.

We went to Oscar's in Encinitas and sat at one of the picnic-style tables. Shortly after our food had been delivered, a young mother and her two children, who appeared to be slightly older than our two kids, sat down in front of us to await delivery of their order. A look of utter disgust came over the young mother's face when she saw my bandage, and she lost no time grabbing her children and moving them to another table where they wouldn't have to look at me. It was the first time I'd ever felt like an outcast; suddenly, I could identify very closely with those who are injured or disabled and have to deal with such intolerance on a regular basis. I can still remember how marginalized I felt. Believe me, it's not a good feeling, nor is it one I'll ever forget.

My eye injury didn't stop me from continuing to play tennis, though. In fact, I played competitively for more than another decade. My lifetime record in tennis finals is 14–4. My last championship occurred in the final competitive match I played at the Lake Murray Tennis Club, in 2009. In reaching those eighteen finals, I had a semifinal record of 18–2. I considered myself a big-match player, just like Bobby Riggs; and, as such, to knock me out of a tournament, an opponent had to get me in the first or second round, because by the third round, I was in my groove.

Thankfully, the surgery to repair my eye was successful, but ongoing treatment required me to keep a layer of protective oil over the eye, which limited my vision to the point that I was still unable to see out of it. As a result, my left eye overcompensated and became dominant. Until October 11, 2001, I functioned with vision in only one eye. Then, on that date, I suffered a spontaneous retinal tear in my left eye while playing tennis at the Lake Murray Tennis Club, of all places. My declining vision became rapidly evident after the practice match, as I drove south to visit my Auntie Bun. She had moved into an assisted-living home in Chula Vista about a year after my Uncle John passed on. By the time I got home from that visit, I had lost more than 50 percent of sight in my left eye. By the next morning, I couldn't see at all. As they say in baseball, I was 0 for 2.

I had sustained multiple retinal tears in my good eye, and now I couldn't see at all. Once again, I found myself needing eye surgery. To make matters even more challenging, scar tissue had formed after my initial surgery, pulling the repair apart again, leaving me with yet another retinal tear. To combat the scar tissue's attempts to return, which would leave me permanently blind in my left eye, I had to be immobilized for ninety straight days, lying on my right side with my head tilted up at a 45-degree angle. I was a prisoner, held hostage by my eyesight, or lack thereof. As you can imagine, there isn't much one can do while in such a position for ninety consecutive—and very long—days, and even if there was, I couldn't see to do it. I could not work and had to file for disability insurance. Naturally, I lost my driver's license. Before it was over, I wound up having five eye surgeries, all done between October 2001 and December 2002. During that time, I couldn't work, exercise or play tennis.

Fortunately, my surgical team—led by lens specialist Dr. William Basuk (who tragically passed away in 2012 at the young age of fifty-one) and lead physician Dr. Robyn Cohen (who has since had to stop practicing due to a disability)—detected that I had become left-eye dominant after losing the sight in my right eye in 1995. That realization opened the door to a treatment plan. They prescribed visual therapy on my right eye during the year I was completely blind in my left eye. Progress was gradual, but the plan worked. Over time, my brain caught on, and I became right-eye dominant and started to regain sight in my right eye early in 2002.

During the year I couldn't exercise, my muscles and my strength disappeared, while the pounds crept on. I was in my early forties and gained forty pounds during my recovery. My newly sedentary life contributed to a diagnosis of high blood pressure and high cholesterol. I was a physical mess, to say the least. By early 2003, after five surgeries, I had regained about 90 percent of my prior vision in my left eye. Through visual therapy, I eventually regained about 80 percent of my original vision in my right eye, though I have subsequently lost it once again due to the scar tissue that has continued to build up over the years. Treating one problem seemed to continually cause another.

Now, I wasn't a bit concerned about having to lose weight. I didn't think it would be too difficult to get down from 230 pounds to, say, 190. I knew how to lose it—cut back on eating and increase physical activity; the weight loss regimen recommended by most doctors. But, reducing the blood pressure and cholesterol was going to be a little trickier. I wasn't fond of taking medications, especially since I'd read the disclosures that accompanied the prescriptions. Some were quite unsettling, as anyone who's seen a pharmaceutical commercial knows. They spend twenty seconds touting the wonder drug of the century, then cram in forty seconds of side effects and warnings, ranging from dizziness and headaches to suicidal thoughts and death. While the meds had mitigated the symptoms of my high blood pressure and cholesterol, they were probably causing all kinds of other health problems that would manifest themselves in the future. No, thank you. I decided I'd rather cure the problem than treat the symptoms.

I expressed my concerns to my primary care physician, Dr. Lawrence Schlitt, and he told me that if I ever wanted to get off the medications, I had to get into shape, and not just tennis shape or baseball pitcher shape. These problems wouldn't go away, Dr. Schlitt said, unless I was really physically fit. Once again, it was time to take decisive action. I had to get out, start moving and embark on a new journey.

Dr. Schlitt's advice turned me into a long-distance runner. He told me to start jogging, and he told me how—jog slowly for five minutes, then walk for five minutes, jog five more, walk five more, and then turn around and repeat the same routine on the way home. It didn't seem like a terribly grueling assignment, and even though I was out of shape, I was anxious to get off the couch. I followed Dr. Schlitt's advice and hit the pavement. Not only did I regain my lost stamina, but also, over the course of 2003, I noticed that the plan was working. My excess weight was falling off, and my blood pressure and cholesterol numbers were improving.

One fortuitous day, after I'd dropped about twenty pounds, my friend, Dan, asked me to join him in a charity 5K race at the Helen Woodward Animal Center. It sounded like a good idea, and it was a cause I supported; one of our dogs was a "rescue" we'd gotten from this great organization. I accepted his invitation and ran my very first 5K in a little more than twenty-five minutes, pushing myself because I didn't want to finish last. My competitive nature had been reignited. And, Dan told me that if I continued losing weight, I could be a really good long-distance endurance runner.

At the time, I was in my mid-forties, but I had not yet encountered that thing called a midlife crisis. Some of my friends were deep into it, with the typical affairs and motorcycles. They were doing stupid things and flirting with a danger I had no desire for—maybe I was too busy lying on a couch and keeping my head at a 45-degree angle to entertain such thoughts. I was more worried about my eyesight than the thought that life was passing me by. Instead, running became my midlife crisis. In 2004, I decided to become a long-distance endurance runner. To accommodate my new hobby, I cut back on tennis, which I had resumed after regaining my eyesight. However, I also resumed playing baseball. To the significant dismay of my eye surgeons, I joined an "over 38" league, which in retrospect I guess you could say was the one dangerous thing I did during my crisis.

Since 2004, I have completed five marathons (26.2 miles) and more than fifty half-marathons (13.1 miles), and I have run countless races of shorter distances. I have won more than twenty gold medals in the 5K distance in my age groups—first forty-five to forty-nine, now fifty to fifty-four—and one half-marathon division championship. I have completed two Boston Marathons, and my personal record is three hours and 54 minutes. My personal half-marathon record is one hour and 40 minutes (Big Sur), and my fastest 5K time is 19 minutes and 53 seconds, for a pace of just under six minutes and 30 seconds per mile.

The strangest thing I've ever done in an attempt to win a gold medal was to intentionally gain seven pounds before running a half-marathon. I attempted this in November 2011, at the Coronado to Imperial Beach "Silver Strand Half." There was logic behind my reasoning, I assure you. You see, I had never won a medal in the half-marathon distance—neither gold nor silver nor bronze. Over shorter distances, I'm rather fast, but at 185 to 190 pounds, I'm considered on the large side for a runner. Experience has shown me it's the smaller runners who win in the longer distances.

If smaller runners usually win, why did I decide to gain weight? Well, the Silver Strand has a "Clydesdale" division for men who weigh 195 pounds and over. I figured I could win a medal in that category—all I had to do was gain a little weight. So I entered the over-forty Clydesdale division and set out to pack on seven pounds in six weeks. I ate pizza every night for six weeks in a row, which I must admit was fun. I weighed in at 196 pounds on race day, one pound over the requirement. Maybe I was enjoying that pizza a little more than I had to.

Did my strategy work? Yes, it did. I ran the half-marathon in one hour and 48 minutes. Competing against thirty-seven other guys in my division, I won the gold! In fact, I was only two minutes behind the under-40 Clydesdale division winner. I might actually be the only runner in history to intentionally gain weight to run in a competition. However, a year later, I was still trying to take the extra weight off, proof that it's easier to gain than to lose. But, you gotta do what you gotta do—and now that I could see, I wanted to do these things.

Cooperation and collaboration were the keys to regaining my eyesight. I had to follow my doctors' orders. And, none of this would have been possible without the support of my wife, Mari; my parents and other relatives; my doctors and surgical teams; and my physical therapists. I believe I have returned this spirit of collaboration through the work that my Move Your Feet Before You Eat Foundation performs in my community.

One person can only do so much, but when multitudes of people collaborate, one plus one can equal more than two. Bobby Riggs was a great collaborator, a fact that surprises almost everyone who hears this statement. Most people regarded him as a self-indulgent egomaniac whose only interest was in taking care of number one.

This perception is simply not true. Bobby's reinvention of himself in 1973 as "king of male chauvinist pigs" and the ultimate Sugar Daddy required great collaboration—with his practice partners and trainers, his nutritionist, his managers and promoters, all kinds of media people, the people he bet with on a variety of events and stunts, and even with his opponents, Margaret and Billie Jean.

As anyone who was fortunate enough to spend time with Bobby will attest, he left significant value behind for everyone with whom he collaborated (even though he probably took your money while doing so). He gave the people around him great publicity and introductions to other interesting people in his circle. First and foremost, however, Bobby always provided a great experience, one you could brag about for the rest of your life.

Gaining weight was the key to getting into a division I could actually win. I called this the "Bobby Riggs training plan," because Bobby was the only other person I'd ever known to gain a bunch of weight before a big competition. Fortunately for me, there were no Billie Jean Kings in my division. Bobby hadn't been so lucky.

Chapter 9

Saving My Best Work for Last

*B*ack in the 1970s, Uncle John had wisely anticipated that the events I was documenting in the scrapbooks would have great historic value. "The material we gather today," he explained, "will have much greater significance for those who want to learn about Bobby Riggs in the future." It was a big responsibility for a mere kid who had never delved into a project of this magnitude, but I gave it my all. In return, I got invaluable lessons, and the knowledge I gained would be called on long after my job was done.

Thirty-nine years after I completed the scrapbooks, James Erskine of New Black Films and his co-producer, Zara Hayes, contacted me. They wanted me to act as a consultant on a documentary film project they were working on with Billie Jean King in anticipation of the fortieth anniversary of the Battle of the Sexes. Billie Jean's intention is that this documentary will serve as a "legacy piece" designed to stand the test of time. I was honored and humbled to be asked to contribute. Thankfully, remembering the events of 1973 was not at all difficult for me, as I have been blessed with a memory that some have described as photographic.

This particular inquiry came in the form of a straightforward question contained in an email from James Erskine: "Do you know who owns the broadcast copyright to the Court vs. Riggs Mother's Day Massacre match?"

Unable to recall any past reference to the owners of the copyright and needing more information before I could adequately research the matter, I turned to common sense. I responded by suggesting that he and his co-producer start with CBS, the network that originally broadcasted the match.

James confirmed that he had indeed assumed that CBS would retain rights to its own material. His inquiry had started with the network. However, CBS representatives informed New Black Films that the network did not, in fact, own the broadcast copyright, and that they didn't know who did.

Upon learning this, I sat quietly in my vegetable garden and searched my brain for any nugget of information that might put us on the proper trail. *This being the case*, I asked myself, *who would most likely be the broadcast copyright owner?* I just knew if I thought long and hard enough, it would come to me. After all, I had read almost everything ever published on the Mother's Day Massacre and the Battle of the Sexes. If anyone knew the answer, it had to be me. But, because I no longer had the scrapbooks, I just had to find it in my memory. As I pondered the possibilities, my memory uncovered and rested on one name—Jackie Barnett.

Jackie Barnett was Bobby Riggs' manager, at least up until one week after the Fourth of July in 1973, when the Battle of the Sexes was introduced to the public. At that point, Jerry Perenchio took over the show (to put it mildly). Jackie was a Hollywood personality manager and had known Bobby for a long time. His client roster included a variety of celebrities, including one client who was arguably more famous than Bobby, namely "The Schnoz," Mr. Jimmy Durante.

Let me shed some light on the man behind the manager: Jackie Barnett took care of one person—himself. He had a reputation for being cheap and never giving anything away. In fact, I discovered from my Uncle John that Bobby made little to no money on the Mother's Day Massacre (other than the money he won by betting on himself) because Jackie Barnett had cut himself such a great deal. Suffice it to say, my uncle didn't like Jackie—and he didn't attempt to keep his feelings to himself. On more than one occasion, I'd heard

Uncle John say, "Jackie has real deep pockets, but he also has real short arms."

With my focus on Jackie as the likely copyright owner, I decided a little research was in order before I shared my suspicions with James Erskine. I went online, entered Jackie's name into a search engine, and—eureka!—I discovered an old newspaper article in the *Rock Hill Herald* archives, written by Don Freeman and dated between the Mother's Day Massacre and the Battle of the Sexes. In this article, Jackie Barnett was quoted saying he not only owned the Court vs. Riggs broadcast rights but that he was also going to be the owner of rights to the upcoming King vs. Riggs extravaganza. It was a smart move on Jackie's part, but not one that panned out as he'd hoped. Jerry Perenchio blocked Jackie's big payday from the Battle of the Sexes, and then Jackie and CBS sued ABC and Perenchio in an attempt to enforce their ownership of the broadcast rights. Ultimately, ownership of the Battle of the Sexes remained with Perenchio and ABC. CBS, disgruntled with the settlement, ran the hit movie *Bonnie and Clyde* opposite ABC's telecast of the Battle of the Sexes.

However, Erskine's inquiry had been about the Mother's Day Massacre, and as far as I could tell, that copyright still remained with Jackie. This presented yet another hurdle. If memory served, Jackie had died long before, so the rightful owner(s) of the copyright was a person or persons unknown. Further research confirmed my recollection. Jackie had passed away on February 27, 1993, in Marina del Rey, a trendy Los Angeles suburb on the shores of the Pacific Ocean. (Bobby passed away two and a half years later.)

I was now back to square one in my quest, but I had one huge asset—my background as a CPA who specialized in estate, gift and trust matters. Based on my experience, I made an assumption: Jackie Barnett had, like most Hollywood types, died without a living trust. If this were the case, his estate would have been administered through probate by the county in which he resided, in this case Los Angeles County. Probate is the process whereby a decedent's estate—namely, his or her assets and liabilities—are administered and distributed, or paid, under the supervision of that county's probate department. Armed with my hypothesis, I knew I, at least, had a good starting point.

I also made a second assumption about the assets Jackie Barnett owned at the time of his passing. Because I was well aware Jackie never gave anything away, I postulated that either he or his production company, Jaybar Productions (which operated under the Columbia umbrella), owned all of the broadcast copyrights Jackie had ever created, regardless of whether they were related to Jimmy Durante, Bobby Riggs, or any other performer or athlete he'd ever represented.

Because Jackie was divorced when he passed, his children were likely to inherit his estate. This conclusion brought me to my last assumption, which was that Jackie's children were like most children of Hollywood types in that they probably had absolutely no interest in keeping their father's considerable amount of "stuff." I knew Jackie had two children, a son and a daughter. His daughter, Dawn, who has been deaf from birth and, at the time of my inquiry, resided in Oregon and confirmed my last assumption. She informed me that neither she nor her brother owned any of their father's old films, television shows or broadcasts. However, she was unable to provide me with any other information or recall any details regarding the administration of her father's estate.

So, I turned my research toward the Los Angeles County Probate Department and learned, to my pleasant surprise, that it possessed in its storage facility all probate records for cases dating back to 1985 (eight years before Jackie Barnett's passing). When I called the department, a very pleasant probate clerk answered the phone, and I proceeded to explain that I wanted to obtain Jackie Barnett's case file. To my excitement, the clerk confirmed that Jackie's case was indeed listed, so my first assumption proved to be correct, too. Two down, one to go.

Following this confirmation, the congenial clerk said, "Now, to be able to give you information on the file, I just need you to confirm the probate case number, please." My heart plummeted to my ankles, and I stammered that I didn't know the case number. I pleaded for the clerk's sympathy, explaining that there was no possible way I could ever get the case number. Rather than shutting me down, she asked politely, "Why is this case of such interest to you?"

My response was obviously the right one. When I explained I was consulting on a film project and told her whom it was for, the probate clerk literally shouted, "Oh my God, Billie Jean King is my hero!" And, although it was against the rules and regulations of the Los Angeles County Probate Department, the helpful clerk said she would do me one favor in an effort to see if she could point me in the right direction.

I had an invaluable source of information on the other end of the line, but only one shot to get the information I needed. I had to be very particular about what I asked for and how I asked for it. I used my one favor wisely. After reciting the five most prominent film and broadcast archive services that buy old films and newsreels from people like Jackie

Barnett's heirs, I asked the probate clerk to please simply review Jackie's file and tell me if the names of any of those five companies appeared in the file.

Three days later, the probate clerk called me back." I can only give you three words," she said. "Historic Films Archive." I nearly fainted. This was precisely the information I needed! The clerk, whose hero was Billie Jean King, became my hero. Historic Films Archive, located in New York, was one of the five companies whose names I had listed.

I immediately emailed James Erskine and Zara Hayes and gave them my incredible findings, so they could contact Historic Films Archive and obtain permission to use the broadcast copyright of Court vs. Riggs in their upcoming documentary. James responded a few days later, not to thank me but to report that we'd hit a dead end. Joe, the owner of Historic Films Archive, had told him that Court vs. Riggs was not on their inventory list. I was heartbroken and not quite ready to accept this news as fact. I immediately logged onto the archive's website, where I found a significant amount of Bobby Riggs material and even more material related to the late Jimmy Durante. It certainly appeared that my second assumption had been correct—Jackie Barnett's heirs had apparently sold their father's collection to Historic Films Archive. The probate file confirmed that the estate transacted business with the archive, and everything else was there. How could Court vs. Riggs not be listed in the inventory? I searched line by line, hoping its omission was merely an oversight, but I had to arrive at the same conclusion. The Mother's Day Massacre simply wasn't there.

I was completely frustrated. How could all these promising clues have led us down the wrong path? There could only be three explanations: Jackie's kids were incorrect, and they did, in fact, still own the rights; Court vs. Riggs had been sold to some other archive service; or, Historic Films Archive actually did own the film but had done a poor job of keeping its inventory list up to date. These were the only logical deductions, given the information I had before me.

As a consultant to the documentary, I was devoutly committed to the cause. I must also admit that my curiosity would not let the disappearance of the film rest. I knew it couldn't have just vanished into thin air. So, I drew on the first lesson I'd received as Bobby Riggs' scrapbook maker: I had to take everything I had and give it all to what I was doing— no matter how frustrating or challenging the task proved itself to be. Also, I reminded myself that the preservation of a legacy was hanging in the balance. Finding the owner of the Court vs. Riggs broadcast rights was essentially a quest to locate a missing piece of American history. If we didn't find it, it would probably be lost for good. So, I told James Erskine to ask Joe, the owner of Historic Films Archive, to search high and low for the film. I was convinced they owned what we were searching for, even though they said otherwise. It was the most obvious conclusion, although I didn't have a great deal of faith that our request would produce any result.

About a week later, I met with James and Zara—we were in San Diego for an interview about the Billie Jean King documentary project. James told me that Joe had found the old film in a box, stored in the recesses of his facility, and was deeply apologetic about the company's poor inventory keeping. Quite possibly for the first time in my life, I was speechless.

Against all odds, we had accomplished our mission. I had taken the knowledge and education I had gained from my days as Bobby Riggs' scrapbook maker, incorporated it with the knowledge and education gained from my CPA career, and used this combination to identify the owner of a lost piece of American history.

The "what ifs" of the situation fascinate me: What if Bobby Riggs' scrapbook maker had not grown up to be a CPA who was an estate, gift and trust expert? What would the outcome have been if I had become a schoolteacher or a fire fighter? Or, what if I had grown up to be a lazy and forgetful person? The trail would have undoubtedly gone cold. This amazing film that captured the Mother's Day Massacre of May 13, 1973, would have remained mislaid in the recesses of an archive. As a result, the most historic, but unremembered, tennis match in the history of the United States would have been lost to posterity.

There is really only one history lesson tennis has ever taught, and this is the lesson we saw playing out in front of our eyes in 1973. While it was their differences that spurred their rivalry on the court, Bobby and Billie Jean's face-off at the Battle of the Sexes signified the beginning of a new relationship between them. Despite their differences, they were able to recognize their similarities. They each had a love for the game that they both played so well. They each were passionate about their beliefs. They were also similar insofar as they both grew up playing tennis on public courts—Billie Jean in Long Beach and Bobby in Los Angeles. Neither played tennis at elite all-white tennis clubs, hitting clean, white tennis balls while wearing stark white clothes and spotless shoes. This similarity in their backgrounds also bonds them together in this history lesson. It is these similarities that enabled them to see that they were, despite their differences, remarkably alike. Thus, they were able to turn a rivalry into a mutual respect and admiration that resulted in a long and enduring friendship. In Billie Jean's book, *Pressure Is a Privilege,* she shares a touching exchange that confirms their bond and pays tribute to their relationship. She reports that in her last conversation with Bobby before his passing, he said, "Billie Jean, we really made a difference, didn't we?"

Yes, indeed, they did. This is why these scrapbooks need to be preserved for generations to come. Legacies such as these never die. They live on for eternity in the lives of those they impact. These scrapbooks connect the dots between where we were then and where we are today. They preserve these legacies so we never forget.

The lessons I learned from my scrapbooking days and my training as a CPA allowed seemingly lost history to be preserved. Billie Jean's defeat of Bobby hadn't put this scrapbook maker out of business, after all. It simply made me save my best work for last.

Chapter 10

Move Your Feet Before You Eat

*I*n 2004, I took up the challenge of reinventing myself, just as Bobby had done more than three decades before. I wasn't hoping to become the "king of male chauvinist pigs," though; I was determined to become a long-distance runner. Because my new hobby contributed to my return to good physical health, long-distance running has meant a lot to me. In early 2006, I decided to share the importance of everyday physical activity and healthy eating with others in my community. So, together with my partner, Kathy Kinane, I co-founded a not-for-profit organization called the Move Your Feet Before You Eat Foundation.

Our foundation centers on the work we do in the town of Oceanside, in San Diego's coastal North County. Oceanside has a lengthy history of gang-related issues and a high rate of multi-generational teen pregnancy. We assist the Oceanside Boys &

Girls Club with after-school running and fitness programs for both private- and public-school students, giving these kids a healthy alternative to activities that would likely get them into trouble. The foundation has also collaborated with Farms to Schools, a group of organic farms in north San Diego County, to encourage elementary schools to grow their own vegetable gardens. Both organizations believe that vending machines full of snack foods are not appropriate in schools.

On Thanksgiving morning, in 2006, we held our first annual Oceanside Turkey Trot, consisting of two 5K races and a series of children's one-mile races. Our first event attracted more than 2,300 runners, and we have grown dramatically since then, having hosted more than 8,300 runners and more than 12,000 people at our finish-line expo for Thanksgiving 2011. We topped 2011's turnout by an additional thousand in 2012, almost quadrupling the number of entrants we had in our first event. Not exactly Battle of the Sexes numbers, but still quite impressive. In total, we raised more than $100,000 for schools and other causes.

At this annual event, you will see three generations of family members—grandparents, parents and children—starting out their Thanksgiving morning by walking or jogging together. Many run in memory of a loved one, some are creating new memories, while others are there to keep family traditions alive. I always run the first race, the five-miler, to get in my serious and competitive run, then I don an eight-pound turkey costume and run the 5K with the extra poundage (maybe I should just wear my turkey costume for my next over-forty Clydesdale race—the weight would come off much easier than it does after six weeks of eating pizza). If nothing else, seeing me run in a turkey costume is definitely worth the entry fee!

Five dollars of every runner's entry fee goes to the charity of the entrant's choice, which is usually one of the schools located in Oceanside. Many schools and other charities use our platform to raise additional funds for themselves. The net profit from the races goes to fund the Oceanside Boys & Girls Club after-school running programs. I'm glad to say that we have raised hundreds of thousands of dollars for local schools and community charities in our short history.

Running in my turkey outfit.

We have been very blessed with a fantastic board of directors, which, in addition to the co-founders, includes Gerry Martin, Roger Martin, Ruben Sandoval, Gary Nessim, and the best finish-line volunteer on the planet, David Cain. They are committed, dedicated and selfless individuals who invest a great deal of their time, talent and energy in our cause, with no compensation. Many also contribute funds for special projects associated with our foundation. The work of the directors is enhanced by the support of our sponsors, who help us reach more people and make a positive impact on programs, schools and the community. Our major sponsors have been Oceanside's largest employer, the cancer-research firm Genentech, and the Pacific Marine Credit Union in Marine Corps Base Camp Pendleton. These sponsors understand what it means to be actively involved in their community. And, lest I forgot, we also have almost 400 volunteers who have bought into our vision for improving the Oceanside community. Many of these volunteers come from the Marine base, and anyone related to a deployed Marine gets to run for free. It's our way of honoring the service of our men and women in uniform.

To see the success of our foundation, just look at the statistics: Since its inception, physical-fitness scores in Oceanside public schools have consistently improved,

Academic Performance Index (API) scores have consistently increased each year, and teen pregnancy is down from its all-time high a few years ago. We have been successful because our focus is not on money but on collaboration. In other words, we believe that community leaders can bring skills, talents and access to networks, and that these resources are scalable, whereas money cannot be scaled ($1 just buys $1 of goods and services).

Indeed, the lessons I learned many years ago as Bobby Riggs' scrapbook maker are being put to good use at the foundation. We put absolutely everything we have into pulling off a seamless, fun and community-oriented event. For example, I jog the five-mile course before that race starts to pick up any trash or palm fronds that have found their way onto the course overnight. But, as we know, it takes a "How can I serve?" attitude to produce the best results, and our community has adopted that mentality. Oceanside's buy-in to our vision is reflected in the tremendous growth in the number of participants. And, we do this collaboratively. The downtown hotel occupancy rate in Oceanside during Thanksgiving the year before our first event was 40 percent; now, it is 100 percent. You cannot get a room unless you reserve one well in advance.

We also hope to create a legacy. After seven amazing years serving the Oceanside community, we cannot foresee any reason why this event cannot continue forever. We will pass the torch onto others, who will keep it burning for future generations, long after our lifetimes. If Bobby Riggs' scrapbooks were the first legacy I created, then the Oceanside Turkey Trot is the second. I am equally proud of both.

As I will discuss in the next chapter, action (or better, participation) is required to bring about positive change in a community. We've found that the single best course of action is getting out and volunteering in the community. Whether you're helping out at a junior tennis tournament, manning a water station or picking up trash at a community 5K, serving the homeless and hungry at a soup kitchen, or delivering food to home-bound seniors, the key is to take action. Good intentions just aren't enough. Without the selfless acts of volunteers, all the good that can be accomplished from intentions and ideas would be for naught.

Collaboration is a significant theme in my foundation's work. When you combine the efforts of almost 400 unpaid volunteers, the support of our sponsors, the running registrants who direct five dollars of their entry fee to the community charity of their choice, and the teams and groups who come out to run and walk together (and who train together before and after the event), you get a great experience—one you can brag about for the rest of your life.

While most people might believe that volunteering is meant only to benefit others, there are secondary benefits that are just as significant. In fact, I've found there are three benefits of community activism and volunteerism (the first of which is obvious): you help make your community a better place to live and work in for all of its members—whether they are directly impacted by your service or not.

The second benefit is not as obvious, but you will agree it exists once you get out and volunteer: You feel better about yourself, regardless of how large or small your contribution was, and any problems you're facing seem less important and stressful.

Benefit number three is typically not mentioned in the context of volunteerism. However, to me, it's profound. This benefit has to do with tolerance. I first understood this benefit during my experience documenting the Mother's Day Massacre and the Battle of the Sexes. While those matches and the swell of public interest that surrounded them were indeed about equality and establishing a level playing field, beneath that there was something much more difficult to break through. The reason so many people had to fight so hard during the civil rights movement of the 1960s and during the women's liberation movement and the Title IX battle of the 1970s is this: underneath inequality exists intolerance. Intolerance is all about keeping people who are different down. I've witnessed intolerance—sometimes involuntary, sometimes willful—throughout my life. I've seen people subjected to discrimination, ridicule, bias and alienation simply because they are different or do not conform to another person's mold.

Before 1973, girls were supposed to grow up to be wives and mothers. If a woman wanted a career, she had two choices: nurse or schoolteacher. Bobby Riggs' comments about women being kept barefoot and pregnant, about their place being in the kitchen and bedroom, would now be considered the epitome of intolerance. But, in 1973 most people accepted them as, at least, somewhat accurate. Behind these remarks, nevertheless, was intolerance.

From the minute we are born, there are differences among us. People are black, white and every color in between. Some are male, and some are female. Some are old, some are young, some are rich, and some are poor. Some believe in God, others do not. Some are gay and some are straight. In this country, there are Democrats, Republicans, Independents and other political affiliations. Republicans blame Democrats, and

Democrats blame Republicans—and I sure hope they both aren't right.

Everybody has his or her own perspective and set of beliefs, but if people who are different cannot learn to coexist successfully, strong communities and legacies are not possible. Both require a joining together for the benefit of the whole. Unfortunately, there will always be inequities and inequalities when intolerance is allowed to exist. This is perhaps the greatest lesson I learned as Bobby Riggs' scrapbook maker, and it's one that I invoke in everything I do.

Thus, the third benefit of community volunteerism is that it serves to break down the barriers erected by intolerance—and unfortunately, there are many. But, as you volunteer, you will find yourself working side by side with people who aren't like you. Perhaps they're of a different gender or have a different color of skin. Perhaps they have a sexual orientation different from yours or hold political or religious beliefs you do not share. Regardless, when you work together toward a common goal—to make the community better for *all*—I believe you will come to understand that there is no room for intolerance. Everybody deserves to be treated respectfully and fairly, and, in many ways, we really aren't very different from each other, after all. We all have feelings, hopes, beliefs and needs. We all have our own passions, skills and talents. Sharing them with others doesn't make them right or wrong. The diversity of our "sameness" makes us special—not different. Furthermore, we are in this thing called "life" together, which is precisely what volunteering is about, working together to make our communities a better place for all who reside and work in them. What better thing can a person do than work to make his or her community a better place? When you do this, everyone benefits, regardless of gender, age, race, physical attributes and beliefs.

People who resist community volunteerism and prefer to stand on their soapbox, howling about how right they are and how wrong everybody else is, will one day stick out like a sore thumb. I attribute this reversal to the young people in our country, who are embracing the opportunity to build better and stronger communities. They are taking action, and they are making a difference. As their numbers grow and their message is shared, those who have opposing views and choose to shout them from the rooftops will dwindle, or at least their voices will have a reduced impact. So, either work to make your community a better place or risk becoming irrelevant in the much more tolerant world that hopefully is our future.

Because I experienced the stigma of being "different" when I had an eye injury, I know the effects of such intolerance. Mine was a temporary affliction, but there are others who face intolerance on a daily basis and at a greater level. I watched and documented the media frenzy as a huge segment of our nation, pitted against each other, took sides to prove or disprove that women were the weaker sex. Strides were made as women won the fight to come out of the kitchen and into the workplace; and yet there, they have had to continue their fight, this time calling for equal pay and advancement. Families have had to fight for acceptance and opportunities for their handicapped children. As a society, we've become more accepting of different races, religions and sexual preferences. I applaud the progress that has been made, but there is still so much to be done. As a father and as a community member, leader and volunteer, this focus is at the heart of everything I do.

Life is a constant battle for territory, and certain powers that be will try to take back ground they've already conceded. Such attempts are evidenced in the attacks on Title IX that occurred about a decade ago, and in the attempted restrictions to female health options that are occurring in a multitude of states today. Furthermore, the lesbian/gay/bisexual/transgender (LGBT) community hasn't yet seen the level of progress made during the civil rights and women's liberation movements. The battle for tolerance, acceptance and equality is not yet over.

I often see this in my work as a CPA. LGBT couples are not afforded certain estate tax benefits that heterosexual married couples have, such as the unlimited marital deduction. Also, LGBT couples are not allowed to file joint income tax returns or access survivor Social Security benefits, even when they share housing, income and possessions just like heterosexual couples. Most states restrict the continuation of pension benefits and health care benefits for LGBT couples, as well. Regardless of one's moral views on homosexuality, there is no reason why "equal protection" should not apply to *all* people in this country. These inequities are borne of intolerance, and the resulting injustices will continue to plague society until people become accepting of our differences.

Of all of the many ironies in the Bobby Riggs story, this is perhaps the best one: he served as a catalyst for reducing intolerance.

For many, Bobby will always be "the guy who lost a tennis match to a girl," but his real legacy is the guts it took to risk everything to prove that women could not compete with men.

Although Bobby lost that bet, he was the only man in 1973 willing to put his money where his mouth was. But, for a man who was willing to take such a great risk, the progress toward a level playing field and the reduction of intolerance would have been slowed down by many years. While this result was certainly not Bobby's intention (remember, he believed Billie Jean could not beat him), it was the result, nonetheless.

The final answer is for people to get out in their communities and take action by volunteering. Jump in and work alongside people who are different from you. Keep an open mind and have some fun—you'll likely find that we aren't all that different, after all. Not only will your community become a better place, but you will also become a better and happier person. You'll recognize that each person— regardless of skin color, gender, political or religious beliefs, and sexual preference—has talents. Every person has feelings and a desire to be accepted for who he or she is. We all have something positive to contribute to our communities; we just have to open our eyes and our hearts and afford everyone the same opportunity to do so. If we do, over time, we will see people for who they are, not "what" they are or are not. In addition, we will see the barriers and roadblocks caused by intolerance become less significant; perhaps someday they will disappear altogether.

Along with Bobby Riggs' scrapbooks, this is the legacy I choose to leave to my family and my community. The Move Your Feet Before You Eat Foundation is the culmination of the lessons I first began to learn as Bobby's scrapbook maker back in 1973. It is the result of the influence that sports and physical activity have had on my life and health, and of a burning desire to eliminate battles between the sexes, the races, the religions, the political affiliations, and the sexual orientations. We all have the responsibility to create this awareness. As a professional athlete, Billie Jean King had that responsibility, too—that's why she accepted Bobby Riggs' challenge. Because women like her and Kathrine Switzer dared to challenge the status quo, women across the world are now free to lace up their shoes and make their mark on the world.

Speaking of which, Move Your Feet Before You Eat co-founder Kathy Kinane has a great Billie Jean King story. While I will respect Kathy's privacy and not disclose her precise age, I will tell you that she is just a bit younger than me. She watched the Battle of the Sexes on television and was so inspired that she immediately convinced her parents to buy her a pair of Billie Jean King's famous blue suede Adidas tennis shoes. Kathy also decided not to accept the status quo, and wearing those tennis shoes, she competed on the boys' cross-country team at her school (there simply wasn't one for girls). Yes, indeed, women have come a long way—many wearing the same blue suede Adidas shoes. They were more than a fashion statement—they were a symbol of the opportunity that Billie Jean King gave women around the world. To this day, those vintage tennis shoes are still among Kathy's prized possessions.

Kathy, Demi and Richard.

Tennis has contributed a great deal to me, to women and to sports. While it's not actually a sport that requires collaboration, there are exceptions—the most obvious being doubles, where each player relies on a partner. The second exception would be Billie Jean King and her partner, Ilana Kloss, and the wonderful accomplishments they're making with their collaborative and team-based World Team Tennis program. So, even while it's not usually a collaborative effort, tennis contributed significantly to our heritage and legacy, especially circa 1973. The Mother's Day Massacre and the Battle of the Sexes taught us something far more profound than who was the best man—or woman. These matches taught us that equal opportunity and fairness are mandatory for cultures and communities to thrive. I hope that, in some small way, my story has contributed to my community and this legacy, inspiring others to move their feet and take action to keep the legacy alive.

Chapter 11

"So, What's Your Play?"

"**O**kay kid, double or nothing," Bobby Riggs challenged me some forty years ago. "So, what's your play?"

I might have only been fifteen, but I wasn't naïve, and I knew where this was going. I'd been around Bobby long enough to understand that he spoke a unique language—a language of betting and gambling. Quickly calculating the odds in his head, he spoke fast, thought fast and moved fast. When he and his practice partner, Lorne Kuhle, would refer to the bets they were placing on an event, they referred to the amounts as "units": "I'll bet you two units the next guy who walks in this room is older than me." I never found out how many dollars one unit equaled, but I suspect it changed on a daily, or even more frequent, basis.

I understood precisely what Bobby was asking me. To be honest, I should have seen it coming. Here's the translation: "Okay kid, double or nothing" meant Bobby wanted to bet the $500 that he owed me. In the end, either I would double my money and get $1,000, or Bobby would keep the $500, and I would get nothing. By the way, this wasn't by any stretch of the imagination a request. Bobby made propositions like this all day long, whenever a financial transaction was involved, and my participation was a given. Saying "No, thank you" was not an option.

When Bobby asked, "So, what's your play?" he was giving me a choice of the game or activity I preferred to gamble on. It was Bobby's way of asking, "What are we going to do to settle the bet?" The question demanded an answer, and a quick one. As I mentioned, my debtor talked fast, and he moved fast. If I hadn't replied just as quickly, he would have taken the choice away from me and chosen the "play" himself. So, I had to think on my feet, somehow accelerating my response while thinking it through. My reply took about only two seconds, but the analysis that went through my head seemed to take much longer. Fortunately, I, too, have always been able to think quickly.

Bobby meant the question literally. I had agreed to put my hard-earned scrapbooking wages on the line, double or nothing. He was a world-renowned tennis star. I wasn't even old enough to drive yet. What was my play going to be?

Trust me, a lot of possibilities went through my head before I answered. My first thought was to shoot free throws with

Bobby. After all, I had played point guard on the freshman basketball team the season before (note that I don't refer to it as the "boys' team." That's because, in 1973, my high school only had a boys' basketball team; the girls' basketball team did not come into being until my senior year—and, by this point in my Battle of the Sexes experience, the significance of that development was not lost on me). While on the team, I had made nineteen out of twenty-seven free throws, which is a little more than a 70-percent success rate. However, I remembered I had once-upon–a-time witnessed Bobby make twenty-four out of twenty-five free throws; his eye-hand coordination was truly quite remarkable. Also, in one of the promotional events leading up to the Battle of the Sexes, Bobby shot free throws with Phoenix Suns all-star guard Dick Van Arsdale and showed impressive accuracy. Realizing the odds weren't in my favor, I quickly took basketball off of my list of options.

Tennis was the easiest game to take off the table. While Bobby would have been more than willing to put eight chairs on his side of the court and wear a raincoat and carry an umbrella in his left hand (a spectacle he'd actually put on many times before) in order to give me a chance, however small, of beating him, I had never touched a tennis racket in my life.

Golf was a definite possibility. I played regularly in high school and had a good long game. However, due to the extended amount of time required to play a round, I ruled out that option, too. Had I opted for golf, our only possibility would have been to hold a putting contest. But, there was one problem—I knew Bobby was a scratch golfer, with an amazing short game (again, due to his eye-hand coordination). In fact, around the time he shot free throws with Dick Van Arsdale in Las Vegas, Bobby also performed well in a putting contest with former boxing champion Joe Louis. So, I ruled that out, as well. It didn't bother me—I still had a couple other options.

My next to last idea was playing cards or some other game of statistical probability with Bobby. But, I knew better than to try this course of action. So, before another nanosecond elapsed, I replied with the last option I had: "Table tennis."

Table tennis (no, I don't call it "ping pong") was the only game I believed I had a remote chance of winning. I had taken it up at my Uncle John's behest when I was just five or six years old. The rest of my family had tried their hands at the sport, and we all fell in love with it.

My family lived in the Bay Area at the time, and whenever we visited Uncle John's house in Sacramento, we played table tennis. Uncle John was so dedicated to it that he always parked his car in the driveway and left the garage to the game. We played for hours on end during those visits. Uncle John was an excellent player and a very good teacher. Me? I was an avid student who spent a lot of time in his garage. Also contributing to the honing of my skills was the fact that my older brother, Bob, took up table tennis with me. Being one year older, Bob was always a little bit better than I was— until I became a teenager.

Bob and I spent a great deal of time with Uncle John and Auntie Bun and the table-tennis table during our childhood. They didn't have any children of their own, so they welcomed us in their home, along with some of Bobby's children, most frequently Larry, who was a good table-tennis player in his own right.

Though we were over there often, it was difficult to master table tennis when we only played on an occasional basis. But, in 1969, when my family moved to Lakeside, Uncle John and Auntie Bun took up residence in Chula Vista, in San Diego County, and later the military town of Coronado, where they didn't have room for a table-tennis table. As fortune would have it, my parents had acquired a home that provided space for one very loved, and very used, such table. Having it in our house gave us an opportunity to play much more often. Now, instead of our family making the trip to Uncle John's house, it was he who frequently made the 30-minute drive from Coronado to our house to play.

My practice wasn't limited to family time, though. By this time, I had also discovered the table-tennis leagues at the beautiful Balboa Park Activity Center near downtown San Diego. The leagues gave me an opportunity to play more often and to test my skills against stiffer competition. So, by the time Bobby Riggs asked me, "So, what's your play?" I had been honing my skills for years. I had even played Bobby a time or two at Uncle John's house. I had my answer. Table tennis was the one and only game I felt I had a chance of beating him at.

Bobby and I had last played table tennis together four or five years earlier. At the time, I was ten, maybe eleven, years old, but I'd been able to compete against him without embarrassing myself. Because I was just a "kid," and I knew Bobby possessed a very short attention span, I suspected he didn't remember our last match and therefore didn't have any inkling of whether I was any good. So, if I had to gamble an entire year's wages, table tennis had to be my game.

But, don't get me wrong—I was hardly overconfident. Bobby was a great athlete, without question. I had watched him compete in table tennis before, and he was good, even impressive. At one point, I even watched him play table tennis against Buddy Blattner, the best table-tennis player I had ever been privileged to watch. Buddy was a former second baseman in major league baseball—later, he became a broadcaster for the St. Louis Cardinals. But, Buddy could have probably also gone pro in table tennis. During World War II, he participated in table-tennis exhibitions at US military bases. Not surprisingly, Buddy won his match against Bobby, but Bobby held his own and was able to keep the score close.

When I informed Bobby that table tennis was my "play," he countered with another question: "So how many points do I have to spot you?" This question was his way of making me believe that my odds of winning the match were reasonable and was, no doubt, based on his assumption that he was the more proficient player. Confidence was not an attribute Bobby lacked, by any stretch of the imagination. In my opinion, his automatic assumption that he would always be crowned the victor was the mistake he made in his battle against Billie Jean King. Whether it would work in his favor against me, I wasn't sure—but we were about to find out. Things became very interesting very quickly when I replied, "I don't need a spot." His eyebrows shot up. I couldn't tell whether he was surprised or impressed, but it was clear that I had gotten his attention.

With those technicalities taken care of, we agreed that we'd play the best two sets out of three. While I had refused a spot, Bobby did give me the advantage of being the first to serve. In table tennis, each player serves five points, alternating always after five serves. The only time that rule didn't apply was when the game was tied at twenty points. In that case, a winner would be announced, after alternating one serve each, when the first player to reach twenty-two or more points also had a lead of at least two points. When Bobby kindly offered me first serve, I took advantage of the small opportunity (like in tennis, I always say it's best to serve first, because to play defense first is a sign that you lack confidence in your own abilities). I grabbed a 4–1 lead and held on for a 21–18 victory.

As always, Bobby was the ultimate competitor, and I knew he would be. He didn't become the best tennis player in the world by overlooking the importance of making adjustments. Sure, his gamesmanship was incredible, but it had to be in order for him to overcome his disadvantages. On the tennis court, he was more often than not the smaller and softer-hitting combatant, and thus Bobby learned early on how important adjustments were to achieving success— in athletics as well as in life. He had proven this point in 1973, when he reinvented himself for the Battle of the Sexes, transforming at age fifty-five from a desk-bound executive and retired tennis pro into the "king of male chauvinist pigs." Yes, Bobby knew how to make adjustments, and with rare exception, those adjustments worked in his favor.

As I played my strategic table-tennis game, Bobby was always ready to counter it, physically and verbally. He thought fast, moved fast and talked even faster. He started talking before the first serve and never stopped during the entire match. He talked so much that I'm surprised he was able to breathe. This tactic could have been part of his strategy, intended to keep me distracted and off my game, but more likely it was just Bobby being Bobby. Either way, I didn't let it get to me. I knew that Bobby was notorious for being a fast-talking hustler—and plus, I was quite accomplished at not listening to adults. Just ask my parents.

As the loser of the first set, Bobby had the option to serve first, and he took it, keeping his advantage because he knew I was for real. If there was ever any doubt in my mind that Bobby was seriously competing against me (and there wasn't), he dispelled it completely in the second set. He had adjusted to my slicing backhand slam shot by moving to his left. As a result, the slice spin arrived at his right-hand paddle, not at his body, where it was intended. Thus, I didn't have as many opportunities to hit winners.

But I, too, knew a little bit about making adjustments. And like Bobby, I also hated to lose, a fact that was evidenced by the paddle-throwing tantrums I sometimes threw when my brother Bob beat me in a match. This was one time, though, when I knew I couldn't let emotions get the better of me. I had to focus on Bobby's game and adjust mine, especially if I wanted to avoid a third set. I noticed Bobby's shift in position, and based on how much territory he was leaving on the right side of his table in order to defend against my backhand slam shot, I opened up my forehand slam to his right side. So, serving and down 17–18, I was able to hold four of my five service points, including breaking a 19–19 tie with a forehand slam winner. Then, I sealed it when I forced an error by Bobby at match point by using a spin serve that I hadn't yet utilized against him. I won! I had beaten the great Bobby Riggs at table tennis, and not only had I won bragging rights—I had also doubled my wages to a cool $1,000! As sweet as the victory was, though, it didn't necessarily mean that my life was about to get any easier. I found that out in very short order.

Bobby paid me with ten $100 bills (he always carried more cash than anybody I'd ever known—enough to make a kid's jaw drop). He was a good sport about losing, too, but I have to admit, if I'd been older, he might have asked for a rematch, double or nothing, to give himself one more shot at winning. He didn't, though, possibly because by this time, it had occurred to him that betting against a fifteen-year-old kid might not have been the most appropriate thing to do. By the way, although I'm quick to point out Bobby's fierce competitiveness and his idiosyncrasies, I'm also willing to give him credit when it's due. If Bobby had won, I knew he wouldn't have let me walk away empty-handed. He wasn't that kind of guy. He would have still handed me $250 or $300, as he would have done with anyone who had done him a great service. But, I'm not so sure my mother would agree.

When my mom picked me up, one of the first things she asked was if I had remembered to get paid. Proudly, I pulled out the pile of $100 bills and proceeded to tell her the story of how it came to be mine. I didn't get very far, though, before I was interrupted. "How many times have I told you not to bet with Bobby? He's a bad influence—all he does is gamble! How could you risk the five hundred dollars?" She went on and on, as mothers do. I tried to defend myself and explain that I hadn't had a choice. It was Bobby's world, and in Bobby's world, you played by Bobby's rules. She should know that. It didn't matter whether I was fifteen years old or forty-five years old—if I had refused to play Bobby, my relationship with Bobby would have been forever changed.

Anyone who chickened out didn't get to stay in Bobby's world. And, although I didn't say it to my mother, I personally believed that Bobby's world was a lot more interesting than anybody else's. I considered myself fortunate to be a part of something so eventful and exciting. Everything else dulled in comparison.

It was quite an eventful day. The scrapbooks were completed and delivered, and I had answered Bobby's challenge successfully. By naming my play, I'd beat Bobby Riggs at table tennis. As a result, I had a tidy $1,000 in my pocket and a harsh tongue-lashing ringing in my ears. The scrapbooks were behind me, but the world around me was changing, and changing fast. And both Bobby Riggs and I were changing, as well.

The Battle of the Sexes without question represented the pinnacle of Bobby's life, and there was very little he did after his loss to Billie Jean that could be considered truly newsworthy, even though he remained in local and regional newspapers for another two or three years as he toured the world as the self-proclaimed "Sugar Daddy."

After his big defeat, interest in Bobby and his act quickly started to wane. On April 10, 1976, his son Jimmy died of an apparent drug overdose on Long Island at age twenty-two. This event, combined with declining post–Battle of the Sexes interest, dramatically slowed Bobby's travel and promotions schedule, then ended it completely. It also no doubt contributed to Bobby reuniting with Priscilla. Bobby became devoted to her in their later years, after they remarried. Once she passed away in 1995, he seemed to lose interest in living and finally succumbed to a lengthy battle with prostate cancer on October 25, 1995, age seventy-seven, in Encinitas, California.

My post-1973 life certainly was even less newsworthy than Bobby's, but perhaps more satisfying in many ways. Still, my time with him had a huge impact on the rest of my life. What I learned from my experiences as a scrapbook maker might surprise you, because I did not learn about what most people assume I did.

That is to say, I did not learn about hard work, determination, preparation and training. While my work on the scrapbooks required these skills, I already possessed an understanding of the importance of these attributes by age fourteen. After all, I was a straight-A student, and wound up being my graduating class' valedictorian. These already-existing traits were the reasons why I was "the man for the job" in the first place.

Well, maybe I did learn a bit about training. I got to witness firsthand how hard Bobby trained for his match against Margaret Court and how it paid off, and then I witnessed Bobby's complete disregard of his training routine prior to his match against Billie Jean and saw the disastrous consequences.

The more important lesson I learned—although I could not have known it in 1973—had to do with the importance of taking action, collaborating and leaving a legacy (actually, let's change *action* to *participation*. In Bobby's world, *action* meant an activity one was betting on—which was pretty much every activity with Bobby—and I don't want to be accused of promoting bad habits).

The result of my focus on these three activities has been amazing, and not at all predictable. Through the Move Your Feet Before You Eat Foundation, I have done all three, and we have managed to decrease the level of intolerance in my community.

Every ending creates a new beginning. When the Battle of the Sexes was over, women across the country experienced a rebirth. As this book ends, I hope it also creates a new beginning for you. I hope you're encouraged to make a positive contribution to your community and your country. Just as Bobby challenged Billie Jean, and then challenged me, I am now posing a challenge to you: take everything you have and give all of it to everything you do, 100 percent, with no exceptions. Find a way to create your own legacy, and get out in your community and volunteer. You, too, can make a difference in someone's life.

I also hope this book puts some of the ongoing conspiracy theories and questions about Bobby Riggs, Billie Jean King, and the Battle of the Sexes and the Mother's Day Massacre to rest.

Speaking of books, my scrapbooks (oops, I said "*my* scrapbooks"...was that a Freudian slip?) presently belong to the Bobby Riggs Tennis Museum Foundation, located in Encinitas, Calif., on Santa Fe Drive, just east of Highway 5. Run by Lorne Kuhle, the museum is an incredible depository of tennis artifacts and memorabilia, including the Sugar Daddy jacket that so irked my Uncle John. Lorne keeps the scrapbooks under lock and key, due to the fragility caused by their advanced age. Ten of the eleven scrapbooks are there—one is missing. Somewhere around 1993, which was the twentieth anniversary of the Battle of the Sexes, Bobby Riggs told me he directed that one of the scrapbooks be sent to the Tennis Hall of Fame in Newport, Rhode Island. However, I have not verified whether that is, indeed, the case.

During the course of this project, I have, on behalf of the foundation, gotten one of the scrapbooks digitized. I plan on doing so for all of them and developing a succession plan for their safekeeping in the future. This is important to me not just because I have a personal connection to them, but also because the scrapbooks are both magical and symmetrical. They present an era when the United States and the world were in a state of upheaval. They represent the most significant and substantial collection of material in existence on this planet surrounding the events of 1973, when Bobby Riggs defeated Margaret Court at the Mother's Day Massacre, and then Billie Jean King defeated Bobby Riggs at the Battle of the Sexes.

During the course of my writing of this book, my sixteen-year-old daughter, Demi, wrote a "reflection" on the legacy of John Steinbeck. What she wrote makes me feel great hope not only for her future, but also for the future of all people who think like this: "Utilize this assignment to learn about someone who changed the way that people think, and appreciate them for acting courageously when all odds were seemingly against them. If we forget who these people are, then 'we are accomplices' (Elie Wiesel). We must not allow future generations to overlook what these people accomplished, because quite possibly they could be the reason we are alive and prospering today."

While I have not dedicated this book to anyone, I certainly intended to do so. There are many deserving people, including Bobby Riggs, Billie Jean King and my family. My initial intention was to dedicate this book to my beloved Mari, Evan, Mia and Demi. However, during the course of writing it, our beloved 150-pound Neapolitan mastiff dog, Beni, had to be put to sleep due to heart problems at the age of nine and a half. In 2003, when I commenced my journey to regain my health, Beni became my very first running partner, and he was a present for Demi on her seventh birthday. Beni, may you joyously run free for the rest of eternity.

I could have dedicated this book to Beni's memory. But, there are others who are gone who also deserve the recognition and remembrance. We have also lost, along the way and in five-year increments: Bobby Riggs in October of 1995, followed by his brother and my uncle, John Riggs, then John's wife, Marion Riggs (Auntie Bun), and last, in May 2010, my father and Marion's brother, Dr. Robert Muscio. They are all dearly missed, but I am pleased to "give you a full report"—as my Uncle John used to ask me to do—that they all left significant legacies behind that shall continue to carry on.

For that reason, there is no dedication, only a moment of silence to pay tribute to them and the legacies that survive them.

Endings become beginnings. The Battle of the Sexes ended a rivalry that turned into the beginning of a long and lasting friendship. My job as Bobby's scrapbook maker became the beginning of a lifetime dedicated to creating awareness of the intolerances among us as I strive to contribute to the betterment of my community.

The end? As it is in legacies, maybe there are no endings.

For you, my reader, maybe this is your beginning—and for that reason, I will leave you with one question to help you get started.

"Okay kid, double or nothing. So, what's your play?"

About the Author

Richard Muscio, CPA, is "THE Family Office Guy." As a CPA with an estate/gift/trust background, Richard assists family offices (ultra-wealthy families) with estate and gift tax planning, family governance and succession planning, with the goal of helping wealthy families to thrive.

Richard speaks frequently on the topics of family governance, professional collaboration, business succession planning, business leaders as community leaders, and "The CPA Firm of the Future." You can view his presentations on these topics on his YouTube channel. He also hosts a weekly radio show, *It's Your Money...and Your Life* (www.iymoney.com) on 760 AM KFMB, where he discusses wealth as being much more than just money.

Richard is co-author of *The Rise* with best-selling author Greg Reid. *The Rise* is about collaboration and never giving up on one's dreams.

He is also co-founder of the Move Your Feet Before You Eat Foundation and the Oceanside Turkey Trot (www.osideturkeytrot.com). His Foundation works to improve teen fitness and senior generation fitness in the Oceanside area, while encouraging family participation and community volunteerism. If you think you had a lot of people over for Thanksgiving, well, Richard hosted more than 9,000 runners and 14,000 people this past Thanksgiving morning in downtown Oceanside, raising more than $100,000 for charities.

For fun, Richard is a long-distance endurance runner, having completed the 2012 Boston Marathon in record-breaking heat. Best of all, Richard is the father of Evan (22), Mia (21) and Demi (17) with his lovely wife, Mari, who enjoys beating him in running events. Richard may be reached via email at rjm@fabcpas.com.